CW00868007

Copyright 2015

License Notes

2016

January, February, March
April, May, June
July, August, September
October, November, December

2017

January, February, March
April, May, June
July, August, September
October, November, December

PERSONAL DETAILS

Name

Address

Telephone Number

Company Name/Number

NHS No

Blood Group

Passport No.

Driving License No.

EMERGENCY Name

EMERGENCY ADDRESS

EMERGENCY TEL No:-

Contents

PERSONAL DETAILS..3

Athletics World Record Times (Men) 5

Athletics World Record Times (Women) 6

CALENDAR OF ATHLETICS EVENTS 2016...7

Diary Of Appointments Starting Monday 28 December 15........................9

End Appointment Diary 1st January 2017 61

HORSE RACING MEETINGS PER DAY 2016...62

Rugby Premier League Fixtures 94

2016 Six Nations fixtures 99

TENNIS TOURNAMENTS 2016 100

Tournament List 100

MAJOR GOLF TOURNAMENTS 2016 104

Past Winners (The Masters) 104

Golf Past Winners (U.S. OPEN) 105

Past Winners (THE. OPEN CHAMPIONSHIP) 105

Past Winners (THE. PGA CHAMPIONSHIP)..106

OTHER GOLF TOURNAMENTS...106

BARCLAYS PREMIER LEAGUE FIXTURES 2016 112

IMPORTANT FOOTBALL CUP FIXTURES..122

Athletics World Record Times (Men)

Distance	Time	Athlete	Country	Date
100 m	9.58	Usain Bolt	Jamaica	19/08/09
200 m	19.19	Usain Bolt	Jamaica	16/08/09
400 m	43.18	Michael Johnson	USA	26/08/99
800 m	01:40.9	David Rudisha	Kenya	09/08/12
1000 m	02:12.0	Noah Ngeny	Kenya	05/09/99
1500 m	03:26.0	Hicham El Guerrouj	Morocco	14/07/98
Mile	03:43.1	Hicham El Guerrouj	Morocco	07/07/99
2000 m	04:44.8	Hicham El Guerrouj	Morocco	07/09/99
3000 m	07:20.7	Daniel Komen	Kenya	01/09/96
5000 m	12:37.4	Kenenisa Bekele	Ethiopia	31/05/04
10,000 m	26:17.5	Kenenisa Bekele	Ethiopia	26/08/05
10km (road)	26:44:00	Leonard Komon	Kenya	26/09/10
1/2 marathon	58:23:00	Zersenay Tadese	Eritrea	21/03/10
Marathon	02:02:57	Dennis Kimetto	Kenya	28/09/14

Athletics World Record Times (Women)

Distance	Time	Athlete	Country	Date
100 m	10.49	Florence G Joyner	USA	16/07/88
200 m	21.34	Florence G Joyner	USA	29/09/88
400 m	47.6	Marita Koch	East Ger	06/10/85
800 m	01:53.3	Jarmila Kratochvílová	Czech	26/07/83
1000 m	02:29.0	Svetlana Masterkova	Russia	23/08/96
1500 m	03:50.0	Genzebe Dibaba	Ethiopia	17/07/15
Mile	04:12.6	Svetlana Masterkova	Russia	14/08/96
2000 m	05:25.4	Sonia O'Sullivan	Ireland	08/07/94
3000 m	08:06.1	Wang Junxia	China	13/09/93
5000 m	14:11.2	Tirunesh Dibaba	Ethiopia	06/06/08
10,000 m	29:31.8	Wang Junxia	China	08/09/93
10km (road)	30:21:00	Paula Radcliffe	GB	23/02/03
1/2 marathon	01:01:54	Florence Kiplagat	Kenya	15/02/15
Marathon	02:15:25	Paula Radcliffe	GB	13/04/03

(INTERNATIONAL ASSOCIATION OF ATHLETICS
FEDERATIONS) & 2016 OLYMPICS

06 May 2016 Doha Meeting
Diamond League Meetings QATAR Doha

Sunday 24th April 2016 LONDON MARATHON

14 May 2016
IAAF Diamond League Shanghai Diamond League
Meetings
PR OF CHINA Shanghai, CHINA

28 May 2016 Prefontaine Classic
Diamond League Meetings UNITED STATES Eugene, OR,
USA

02 June 2016 Golden Gala
Diamond League Meetings ITALY Roma,ITALY

05 June 2016 Birmingham Grand Prix
Diamond League Meetings GB & N.I. Birmingham

09 June 2016 ExxonMobil Bislett Games
Diamond League Meetings Oslo,NORWAY

16 June 2016 Stockholm Bauhaus Athletics
Diamond League Meetings Stockholm, SWEDEN

18 June 2016
Adidas Grand Prix New York Diamond League Meetings
NY, USA

15 July 2016 Herculis
Diamond League Meetings MONACO

22 JUL 2016 - 23 JUL 2016 London Grand Prix Diamond
League Meetings GB & N.I. Birmingham

**5/8/2016 - 23/8/2016 OLYMPIC GAMES 2016 Rio de
Janeiro   BRAZIL**

25 August 2016 Athletissima Lausanne Diamond League
Meetings Lausanne, SWITZERLAND

27 August 2016 Meeting Paris
Diamond League Meetings Paris Saint-Denis, FRANCE

01 September 2016 Weltklasse Zürich Diamond League
Meetings Zürich, SWITZERLAND

09 September 2016 AG Memorial van Damme
Diamond League Meetings Bruxelles, BELGIUM

- to Sunday 03 January 16

			M	T	W	T	F	S	S
Important		Appointments							
	8	:00							
		:15							
		:30							
		:45							
	9	:00							
		:15							
		:30							
		:45							
	10	:00							
Priority Tasks		:15							
		:30							
		:45							
	11	:00							
		:15							
		:30							
		:45							
	12	:00							
		:15							
		:30							
		:45							
	1	:00							
		:15							
		:30							
		:45							
	2	:00							
		:15							
		:30							
Time		:45							
	3	:00							
		:15							
		:30							
		:45							
	4	:00							
		:15							
		:30							
		:45							
	5	:00							
£		:30							
	6	:00							
		:30							
	7	:00							
		:30							
	8	:00							

Important			M	T	W	T	F	S	S
	8	:00							
		:15							
		:30							
		:45							
	9	:00							
		:15							
		:30							
		:45							
	10	:00							
Priority Tasks		:15							
		:30							
		:45							
	11	:00							
		:15							
		:30							
		:45							
	12	:00							
		:15							
		:30							
		:45							
	1	:00							
		:15							
		:30							
		:45							
	2	:00							
		:15							
		:30							
Time		:45							
	3	:00							
		:15							
		:30							
		:45							
	4	:00							
		:15							
		:30							
		:45							
	5	:00							
£		:30							
	6	:00							
		:30							
	7	:00							
		:30							
	8	:00							

Appointments

Important			M	T	W	T	F	S	S
	8	:00							
		:15							
		:30							
		:45							
	9	:00							
		:15							
		:30							
		:45							
	10	:00							
Priority Tasks		:15							
		:30							
		:45							
	11	:00							
		:15							
		:30							
		:45							
	12	:00							
		:15							
		:30							
		:45							
	1	:00							
		:15							
		:30							
		:45							
	2	:00							
		:15							
		:30							
Time		:45							
	3	:00							
		:15							
		:30							
		:45							
	4	:00							
		:15							
		:30							
		:45							
	5	:00							
£		:30							
	6	:00							
		:30							
	7	:00							
		:30							
	8	:00							

Monday 18 January 16 - Sunday 24 January 16

Important		Appointments	M	T	W	T	F	S	S
	8 :00								
	:15								
	:30								
	:45								
	9 :00								
	:15								
	:30								
	:45								
Priority Tasks	10 :00								
	:15								
	:30								
	:45								
	11 :00								
	:15								
	:30								
	:45								
	12 :00								
	:15								
	:30								
	:45								
	1 :00								
	:15								
	:30								
	:45								
	2 :00								
	:15								
	:30								
Time	:45								
	3 :00								
	:15								
	:30								
	:45								
	4 :00								
	:15								
	:30								
	:45								
	5 :00								
	:30								
£	6 :00								
	:30								
	7 :00								
	:30								
	8 :00								

Important				Appointments					
			M	T	W	T	F	S	S
	8	:00							
		:15							
		:30							
		:45							
	9	:00							
		:15							
		:30							
		:45							
	10	:00							
Priority Tasks		:15							
		:30							
		:45							
	11	:00							
		:15							
		:30							
		:45							
	12	:00							
		:15							
		:30							
		:45							
	1	:00							
		:15							
		:30							
		:45							
	2	:00							
		:15							
		:30							
Time		:45							
	3	:00							
		:15							
		:30							
		:45							
	4	:00							
		:15							
		:30							
		:45							
	5	:00							
£		:30							
	6	:00							
		:30							
	7	:00							
		:30							
	8	:00							

Appointments

Important			M	T	W	T	F	S	S
	8	:00							
		:15							
		:30							
		:45							
	9	:00							
		:15							
		:30							
		:45							
	10	:00							
Priority Tasks		:15							
		:30							
		:45							
	11	:00							
		:15							
		:30							
		:45							
	12	:00							
		:15							
		:30							
		:45							
	1	:00							
		:15							
		:30							
		:45							
	2	:00							
		:15							
		:30							
Time		:45							
	3	:00							
		:15							
		:30							
		:45							
	4	:00							
		:15							
		:30							
		:45							
	5	:00							
£		:30							
	6	:00							
		:30							
	7	:00							
		:30							
	8	:00							

Important		Appointments						
		M	T	W	T	F	S	S
	8 :00							
	:15							
	:30							
	:45							
	9 :00							
	:15							
	:30							
	:45							
	10 :00							
Priority Tasks	:15							
	:30							
	:45							
	11 :00							
	:15							
	:30							
	:45							
	12 :00							
	:15							
	:30							
	:45							
	1 :00							
	:15							
	:30							
	:45							
	2 :00							
	:15							
	:30							
Time	:45							
	3 :00							
	:15							
	:30							
	:45							
	4 :00							
	:15							
	:30							
	:45							
	5 :00							
£	:30							
	6 :00							
	:30							
	7 :00							
	:30							
	8 :00							

Important			M	T	W	T	F	S	S
	8	:00							
		:15							
		:30							
		:45							
	9	:00							
		:15							
		:30							
		:45							
Priority Tasks	10	:00							
		:15							
		:30							
		:45							
	11	:00							
		:15							
		:30							
		:45							
	12	:00							
		:15							
		:30							
		:45							
	1	:00							
		:15							
		:30							
		:45							
	2	:00							
		:15							
		:30							
Time		:45							
	3	:00							
		:15							
		:30							
		:45							
	4	:00							
		:15							
		:30							
		:45							
	5	:00							
£		:30							
	6	:00							
		:30							
	7	:00							
		:30							
	8	:00							

Appointments

Important		Appointments						
		M	T	W	T	F	S	S
	8 :00							
	:15							
	:30							
	:45							
	9 :00							
	:15							
	:30							
	:45							
	10 :00							
Priority Tasks	:15							
	:30							
	:45							
	11 :00							
	:15							
	:30							
	:45							
	12 :00							
	:15							
	:30							
	:45							
	1 :00							
	:15							
	:30							
	:45							
	2 :00							
	:15							
	:30							
Time	:45							
	3 :00							
	:15							
	:30							
	:45							
	4 :00							
	:15							
	:30							
	:45							
	5 :00							
£	:30							
	6 :00							
	:30							
	7 :00							
	:30							
	8 :00							

Important			M	T	W	T	F	S	S
	8	:00							
		:15							
		:30							
		:45							
	9	:00							
		:15							
		:30							
		:45							
	10	:00							
Priority Tasks		:15							
		:30							
		:45							
	11	:00							
		:15							
		:30							
		:45							
	12	:00							
		:15							
		:30							
		:45							
	1	:00							
		:15							
		:30							
		:45							
	2	:00							
		:15							
		:30							
Time		:45							
	3	:00							
		:15							
		:30							
		:45							
	4	:00							
		:15							
		:30							
		:45							
	5	:00							
£		:30							
	6	:00							
		:30							
	7	:00							
		:30							
	8	:00							

			Appointments						
Important			**M**	**T**	**W**	**T**	**F**	**S**	**S**
	8	:00							
		:15							
		:30							
		:45							
	9	:00							
		:15							
		:30							
		:45							
	10	:00							
Priority Tasks		:15							
		:30							
		:45							
	11	:00							
		:15							
		:30							
		:45							
	12	:00							
		:15							
		:30							
		:45							
	1	:00							
		:15							
		:30							
		:45							
	2	:00							
		:15							
		:30							
Time		:45							
	3	:00							
		:15							
		:30							
		:45							
	4	:00							
		:15							
		:30							
		:45							
	5	:00							
£		:30							
	6	:00							
		:30							
	7	:00							
		:30							
	8	:00							

Monday 14 March 16 - Sunday 20 March 16

				Appointments					
Important			M	T	W	T	F	S	S
	8	:00							
		:15							
		:30							
		:45							
	9	:00							
		:15							
		:30							
		:45							
	10	:00							
Priority Tasks		:15							
		:30							
		:45							
	11	:00							
		:15							
		:30							
		:45							
	12	:00							
		:15							
		:30							
		:45							
	1	:00							
		:15							
		:30							
		:45							
	2	:00							
		:15							
		:30							
Time		:45							
	3	:00							
		:15							
		:30							
		:45							
	4	:00							
		:15							
		:30							
		:45							
	5	:00							
£		:30							
	6	:00							
		:30							
	7	:00							
		:30							
	8	:00							

Monday 21 March 16 - Sunday 27 March 16

Important				M	T	W	T	F	S	S
	8	:00								
		:15								
		:30								
		:45								
	9	:00								
		:15								
		:30								
		:45								
	10	:00								
Priority Tasks		:15								
		:30								
		:45								
	11	:00								
		:15								
		:30								
		:45								
	12	:00								
		:15								
		:30								
		:45								
	1	:00								
		:15								
		:30								
		:45								
	2	:00								
		:15								
		:30								
Time		:45								
	3	:00								
		:15								
		:30								
		:45								
	4	:00								
		:15								
		:30								
		:45								
	5	:00								
£		:30								
	6	:00								
		:30								
	7	:00								
		:30								
	8	:00								

Appointments

Important			Appointments						
			M	T	W	T	F	S	S
	8	:00							
		:15							
		:30							
		:45							
	9	:00							
		:15							
		:30							
		:45							
	10	:00							
Priority Tasks		:15							
		:30							
		:45							
	11	:00							
		:15							
		:30							
		:45							
	12	:00							
		:15							
		:30							
		:45							
	1	:00							
		:15							
		:30							
		:45							
	2	:00							
		:15							
		:30							
Time		:45							
	3	:00							
		:15							
		:30							
		:45							
	4	:00							
		:15							
		:30							
		:45							
	5	:00							
£		:30							
	6	:00							
		:30							
	7	:00							
		:30							
	8	:00							

Important			Appointments						
			M	T	W	T	F	S	S
	8	:00							
		:15							
		:30							
		:45							
	9	:00							
		:15							
		:30							
		:45							
	10	:00							
Priority Tasks		:15							
		:30							
		:45							
	11	:00							
		:15							
		:30							
		:45							
	12	:00							
		:15							
		:30							
		:45							
	1	:00							
		:15							
		:30							
		:45							
	2	:00							
		:15							
		:30							
Time		:45							
	3	:00							
		:15							
		:30							
		:45							
	4	:00							
		:15							
		:30							
		:45							
	5	:00							
£		:30							
	6	:00							
		:30							
	7	:00							
		:30							
	8	:00							

Important				Appointments						
			M	T	W	T	F	S	S
	8	:00							
		:15							
		:30							
		:45							
	9	:00							
		:15							
		:30							
		:45							
	10	:00							
Priority Tasks		:15							
		:30							
		:45							
	11	:00							
		:15							
		:30							
		:45							
	12	:00							
		:15							
		:30							
		:45							
	1	:00							
		:15							
		:30							
		:45							
	2	:00							
		:15							
		:30							
Time		:45							
	3	:00							
		:15							
		:30							
		:45							
	4	:00							
		:15							
		:30							
		:45							
	5	:00							
£		:30							
	6	:00							
		:30							
	7	:00							
		:30							
	8	:00							

Important			M	T	W	T	F	S	S
	8	:00							
		:15							
		:30							
		:45							
	9	:00							
		:15							
		:30							
		:45							
	10	:00							
Priority Tasks		:15							
		:30							
		:45							
	11	:00							
		:15							
		:30							
		:45							
	12	:00							
		:15							
		:30							
		:45							
	1	:00							
		:15							
		:30							
		:45							
	2	:00							
		:15							
		:30							
Time		:45							
	3	:00							
		:15							
		:30							
		:45							
	4	:00							
		:15							
		:30							
		:45							
	5	:00							
£		:30							
	6	:00							
		:30							
	7	:00							
		:30							
	8	:00							

Appointments

Monday 25 April 16 - Sunday 01 May 16

Important			M	T	W	T	F	S	S
	8	:00							
		:15							
		:30							
		:45							
	9	:00							
		:15							
		:30							
		:45							
	10	:00							
Priority Tasks		:15							
		:30							
		:45							
	11	:00							
		:15							
		:30							
		:45							
	12	:00							
		:15							
		:30							
		:45							
	1	:00							
		:15							
		:30							
		:45							
	2	:00							
		:15							
		:30							
Time		:45							
	3	:00							
		:15							
		:30							
		:45							
	4	:00							
		:15							
		:30							
		:45							
	5	:00							
£		:30							
	6	:00							
		:30							
	7	:00							
		:30							
	8	:00							

Appointments

Important			Appointments					
		M	T	W	T	F	S	S
	8 :00							
	:15							
	:30							
	:45							
	9 :00							
	:15							
	:30							
	:45							
	10 :00							
Priority Tasks	:15							
	:30							
	:45							
	11 :00							
	:15							
	:30							
	:45							
	12 :00							
	:15							
	:30							
	:45							
	1 :00							
	:15							
	:30							
	:45							
	2 :00							
	:15							
	:30							
Time	:45							
	3 :00							
	:15							
	:30							
	:45							
	4 :00							
	:15							
	:30							
	:45							
	5 :00							
£	:30							
	6 :00							
	:30							
	7 :00							
	:30							
	8 :00							

Important			Appointments						
			M	T	W	T	F	S	S
	8	:00							
		:15							
		:30							
		:45							
	9	:00							
		:15							
		:30							
		:45							
	10	:00							
Priority Tasks		:15							
		:30							
		:45							
	11	:00							
		:15							
		:30							
		:45							
	12	:00							
		:15							
		:30							
		:45							
	1	:00							
		:15							
		:30							
		:45							
	2	:00							
		:15							
		:30							
Time		:45							
	3	:00							
		:15							
		:30							
		:45							
	4	:00							
		:15							
		:30							
		:45							
	5	:00							
£		:30							
	6	:00							
		:30							
	7	:00							
		:30							
	8	:00							

Monday 16 May 16 - Sunday 22 May 16

Important			M	T	W	T	F	S	S
	8	:00							
		:15							
		:30							
		:45							
	9	:00							
		:15							
		:30							
		:45							
	10	:00							
Priority Tasks		:15							
		:30							
		:45							
	11	:00							
		:15							
		:30							
		:45							
	12	:00							
		:15							
		:30							
		:45							
	1	:00							
		:15							
		:30							
		:45							
	2	:00							
		:15							
		:30							
Time		:45							
	3	:00							
		:15							
		:30							
		:45							
	4	:00							
		:15							
		:30							
		:45							
	5	:00							
£		:30							
	6	:00							
		:30							
	7	:00							
		:30							
	8	:00							

Important			M	T	W	T	F	S	S
	8	:00							
		:15							
		:30							
		:45							
	9	:00							
		:15							
		:30							
		:45							
	10	:00							
Priority Tasks		:15							
		:30							
		:45							
	11	:00							
		:15							
		:30							
		:45							
	12	:00							
		:15							
		:30							
		:45							
	1	:00							
		:15							
		:30							
		:45							
	2	:00							
		:15							
		:30							
Time		:45							
	3	:00							
		:15							
		:30							
		:45							
	4	:00							
		:15							
		:30							
		:45							
	5	:00							
£		:30							
	6	:00							
		:30							
	7	:00							
		:30							
	8	:00							

Appointments

Important			Appointments						
			M	**T**	**W**	**T**	**F**	**S**	**S**
	8	:00							
		:15							
		:30							
		:45							
	9	:00							
		:15							
		:30							
		:45							
	10	:00							
Priority Tasks		:15							
		:30							
		:45							
	11	:00							
		:15							
		:30							
		:45							
	12	:00							
		:15							
		:30							
		:45							
	1	:00							
		:15							
		:30							
		:45							
	2	:00							
		:15							
		:30							
Time		:45							
	3	:00							
		:15							
		:30							
		:45							
	4	:00							
		:15							
		:30							
		:45							
	5	:00							
£		:30							
	6	:00							
		:30							
	7	:00							
		:30							
	8	:00							

Important			M	T	W	T	F	S	S
	8	:00							
		:15							
		:30							
		:45							
	9	:00							
		:15							
		:30							
		:45							
	10	:00							
Priority Tasks		:15							
		:30							
		:45							
	11	:00							
		:15							
		:30							
		:45							
	12	:00							
		:15							
		:30							
		:45							
	1	:00							
		:15							
		:30							
		:45							
	2	:00							
		:15							
		:30							
Time		:45							
	3	:00							
		:15							
		:30							
		:45							
	4	:00							
		:15							
		:30							
		:45							
	5	:00							
£		:30							
	6	:00							
		:30							
	7	:00							
		:30							
	8	:00							

Important			M	T	W	T	F	S	S
	8	:00							
		:15							
		:30							
		:45							
	9	:00							
		:15							
		:30							
		:45							
Priority Tasks	10	:00							
		:15							
		:30							
		:45							
	11	:00							
		:15							
		:30							
		:45							
	12	:00							
		:15							
		:30							
		:45							
	1	:00							
		:15							
		:30							
		:45							
	2	:00							
		:15							
		:30							
Time		:45							
	3	:00							
		:15							
		:30							
		:45							
	4	:00							
		:15							
		:30							
		:45							
	5	:00							
£		:30							
	6	:00							
		:30							
	7	:00							
		:30							
	8	:00							

Important			M	T	W	T	F	S	S
	8	:00							
		:15							
		:30							
		:45							
	9	:00							
		:15							
		:30							
		:45							
	10	:00							
Priority Tasks		:15							
		:30							
		:45							
	11	:00							
		:15							
		:30							
		:45							
	12	:00							
		:15							
		:30							
		:45							
	1	:00							
		:15							
		:30							
		:45							
	2	:00							
		:15							
		:30							
Time		:45							
	3	:00							
		:15							
		:30							
		:45							
	4	:00							
		:15							
		:30							
		:45							
	5	:00							
£		:30							
	6	:00							
		:30							
	7	:00							
		:30							
	8	:00							

Important			M	T	W	T	F	S	S
	8	:00							
		:15							
		:30							
		:45							
	9	:00							
		:15							
		:30							
		:45							
	10	:00							
Priority Tasks		:15							
		:30							
		:45							
	11	:00							
		:15							
		:30							
		:45							
	12	:00							
		:15							
		:30							
		:45							
	1	:00							
		:15							
		:30							
		:45							
	2	:00							
		:15							
		:30							
Time		:45							
	3	:00							
		:15							
		:30							
		:45							
	4	:00							
		:15							
		:30							
		:45							
	5	:00							
£		:30							
	6	:00							
		:30							
	7	:00							
		:30							
	8	:00							

Appointments

Important				M	T	W	T	F	S	S
		8	:00							
			:15							
			:30							
			:45							
		9	:00							
			:15							
			:30							
			:45							
		10	:00							
Priority Tasks			:15							
			:30							
			:45							
		11	:00							
			:15							
			:30							
			:45							
		12	:00							
			:15							
			:30							
			:45							
		1	:00							
			:15							
			:30							
			:45							
		2	:00							
			:15							
			:30							
Time			:45							
		3	:00							
			:15							
			:30							
			:45							
		4	:00							
			:15							
			:30							
			:45							
		5	:00							
£			:30							
		6	:00							
			:30							
		7	:00							
			:30							
		8	:00							

Appointments

			Appointments						
Important			M	T	W	T	F	S	S
	8	:00							
		:15							
		:30							
		:45							
	9	:00							
		:15							
		:30							
		:45							
	10	:00							
Priority Tasks		:15							
		:30							
		:45							
	11	:00							
		:15							
		:30							
		:45							
	12	:00							
		:15							
		:30							
		:45							
	1	:00							
		:15							
		:30							
		:45							
	2	:00							
		:15							
		:30							
Time		:45							
	3	:00							
		:15							
		:30							
		:45							
	4	:00							
		:15							
		:30							
		:45							
	5	:00							
£		:30							
	6	:00							
		:30							
	7	:00							
		:30							
	8	:00							

Important				Appointments						
				M	T	W	T	F	S	S
	8	:00								
		:15								
		:30								
		:45								
	9	:00								
		:15								
		:30								
		:45								
	10	:00								
Priority Tasks		:15								
		:30								
		:45								
	11	:00								
		:15								
		:30								
		:45								
	12	:00								
		:15								
		:30								
		:45								
	1	:00								
		:15								
		:30								
		:45								
	2	:00								
		:15								
		:30								
Time		:45								
	3	:00								
		:15								
		:30								
		:45								
	4	:00								
		:15								
		:30								
		:45								
	5	:00								
£		:30								
	6	:00								
		:30								
	7	:00								
		:30								
	8	:00								

Important			M	T	W	T	F	S	S
	8	:00							
		:15							
		:30							
		:45							
	9	:00							
		:15							
		:30							
		:45							
	10	:00							
Priority Tasks		:15							
		:30							
		:45							
	11	:00							
		:15							
		:30							
		:45							
	12	:00							
		:15							
		:30							
		:45							
	1	:00							
		:15							
		:30							
		:45							
	2	:00							
		:15							
		:30							
Time		:45							
	3	:00							
		:15							
		:30							
		:45							
	4	:00							
		:15							
		:30							
		:45							
	5	:00							
£		:30							
	6	:00							
		:30							
	7	:00							
		:30							
	8	:00							

Appointments

			Appointments					
Important		M	T	W	T	F	S	S
	8 :00							
	:15							
	:30							
	:45							
	9 :00							
	:15							
	:30							
	:45							
	10 :00							
Priority Tasks	:15							
	:30							
	:45							
	11 :00							
	:15							
	:30							
	:45							
	12 :00							
	:15							
	:30							
	:45							
	1 :00							
	:15							
	:30							
	:45							
	2 :00							
	:15							
	:30							
Time	:45							
	3 :00							
	:15							
	:30							
	:45							
	4 :00							
	:15							
	:30							
	:45							
	5 :00							
£	:30							
	6 :00							
	:30							
	7 :00							
	:30							
	8 :00							

			Appointments						
Important			M	T	W	T	F	S	S
	8	:00							
		:15							
		:30							
		:45							
	9	:00							
		:15							
		:30							
		:45							
	10	:00							
Priority Tasks		:15							
		:30							
		:45							
	11	:00							
		:15							
		:30							
		:45							
	12	:00							
		:15							
		:30							
		:45							
	1	:00							
		:15							
		:30							
		:45							
	2	:00							
		:15							
		:30							
Time		:45							
	3	:00							
		:15							
		:30							
		:45							
	4	:00							
		:15							
		:30							
		:45							
	5	:00							
£		:30							
	6	:00							
		:30							
	7	:00							
		:30							
	8	:00							

			Appointments						
Important			**M**	**T**	**W**	**T**	**F**	**S**	**S**
	8	:00							
		:15							
		:30							
		:45							
	9	:00							
		:15							
		:30							
		:45							
	10	:00							
Priority Tasks		:15							
		:30							
		:45							
	11	:00							
		:15							
		:30							
		:45							
	12	:00							
		:15							
		:30							
		:45							
	1	:00							
		:15							
		:30							
		:45							
	2	:00							
		:15							
		:30							
Time		:45							
	3	:00							
		:15							
		:30							
		:45							
	4	:00							
		:15							
		:30							
		:45							
	5	:00							
£		:30							
	6	:00							
		:30							
	7	:00							
		:30							
	8	:00							

Important			Appointments						
			M	T	W	T	F	S	S
	8	:00							
		:15							
		:30							
		:45							
	9	:00							
		:15							
		:30							
		:45							
	10	:00							
Priority Tasks		:15							
		:30							
		:45							
	11	:00							
		:15							
		:30							
		:45							
	12	:00							
		:15							
		:30							
		:45							
	1	:00							
		:15							
		:30							
		:45							
	2	:00							
		:15							
		:30							
Time		:45							
	3	:00							
		:15							
		:30							
		:45							
	4	:00							
		:15							
		:30							
		:45							
	5	:00							
£		:30							
	6	:00							
		:30							
	7	:00							
		:30							
	8	:00							

Important		Appointments						
		M	T	W	T	F	S	S
	8 :00							
	:15							
	:30							
	:45							
	9 :00							
	:15							
	:30							
	:45							
	10 :00							
Priority Tasks	:15							
	:30							
	:45							
	11 :00							
	:15							
	:30							
	:45							
	12 :00							
	:15							
	:30							
	:45							
	1 :00							
	:15							
	:30							
	:45							
	2 :00							
	:15							
	:30							
Time	:45							
	3 :00							
	:15							
	:30							
	:45							
	4 :00							
	:15							
	:30							
	:45							
	5 :00							
£	:30							
	6 :00							
	:30							
	7 :00							
	:30							
	8 :00							

Important			M	T	W	T	F	S	S
	8	:00							
		:15							
		:30							
		:45							
	9	:00							
		:15							
		:30							
		:45							
Priority Tasks	10	:00							
		:15							
		:30							
		:45							
	11	:00							
		:15							
		:30							
		:45							
	12	:00							
		:15							
		:30							
		:45							
	1	:00							
		:15							
		:30							
		:45							
	2	:00							
		:15							
		:30							
Time		:45							
	3	:00							
		:15							
		:30							
		:45							
	4	:00							
		:15							
		:30							
		:45							
	5	:00							
£		:30							
	6	:00							
		:30							
	7	:00							
		:30							
	8	:00							

Appointments

Important			M	T	W	T	F	S	S
	8	:00							
		:15							
		:30							
		:45							
	9	:00							
		:15							
		:30							
		:45							
	10	:00							
Priority Tasks		:15							
		:30							
		:45							
	11	:00							
		:15							
		:30							
		:45							
	12	:00							
		:15							
		:30							
		:45							
	1	:00							
		:15							
		:30							
		:45							
	2	:00							
		:15							
		:30							
Time		:45							
	3	:00							
		:15							
		:30							
		:45							
	4	:00							
		:15							
		:30							
		:45							
	5	:00							
£		:30							
	6	:00							
		:30							
	7	:00							
		:30							
	8	:00							

Appointments

Monday 19 September 16 - Sunday 25 September 16

Important			M	T	W	T	F	S	S
						Appointments			
	8	:00							
		:15							
		:30							
		:45							
	9	:00							
		:15							
		:30							
		:45							
	10	:00							
Priority Tasks		:15							
		:30							
		:45							
	11	:00							
		:15							
		:30							
		:45							
	12	:00							
		:15							
		:30							
		:45							
	1	:00							
		:15							
		:30							
		:45							
	2	:00							
		:15							
		:30							
Time		:45							
	3	:00							
		:15							
		:30							
		:45							
	4	:00							
		:15							
		:30							
		:45							
	5	:00							
£		:30							
	6	:00							
		:30							
	7	:00							
		:30							
	8	:00							

Important			Appointments						
			M	T	W	T	F	S	S
	8	:00							
		:15							
		:30							
		:45							
	9	:00							
		:15							
		:30							
		:45							
	10	:00							
Priority Tasks		:15							
		:30							
		:45							
	11	:00							
		:15							
		:30							
		:45							
	12	:00							
		:15							
		:30							
		:45							
	1	:00							
		:15							
		:30							
		:45							
	2	:00							
		:15							
		:30							
Time		:45							
	3	:00							
		:15							
		:30							
		:45							
	4	:00							
		:15							
		:30							
		:45							
	5	:00							
£		:30							
	6	:00							
		:30							
	7	:00							
		:30							
	8	:00							

			Appointments					
Important			**M**	**T**	**W**	**T**	**F**	**S**	**S**

Important			M	T	W	T	F	S	S
	8	:00							
		:15							
		:30							
		:45							
	9	:00							
		:15							
		:30							
		:45							
	10	:00							
Priority Tasks		:15							
		:30							
		:45							
	11	:00							
		:15							
		:30							
		:45							
	12	:00							
		:15							
		:30							
		:45							
	1	:00							
		:15							
		:30							
		:45							
	2	:00							
		:15							
		:30							
Time		:45							
	3	:00							
		:15							
		:30							
		:45							
	4	:00							
		:15							
		:30							
		:45							
	5	:00							
£		:30							
	6	:00							
		:30							
	7	:00							
		:30							
	8	:00							

		Appointments						
Important		**M**	**T**	**W**	**T**	**F**	**S**	**S**
	8 :00							
	:15							
	:30							
	:45							
	9 :00							
	:15							
	:30							
	:45							
	10 :00							
Priority Tasks	:15							
	:30							
	:45							
	11 :00							
	:15							
	:30							
	:45							
	12 :00							
	:15							
	:30							
	:45							
	1 :00							
	:15							
	:30							
	:45							
	2 :00							
	:15							
	:30							
Time	:45							
	3 :00							
	:15							
	:30							
	:45							
	4 :00							
	:15							
	:30							
	:45							
	5 :00							
£	:30							
	6 :00							
	:30							
	7 :00							
	:30							
	8 :00							

Important			M	T	W	T	F	S	S
	8	:00							
		:15							
		:30							
		:45							
	9	:00							
		:15							
		:30							
		:45							
	10	:00							
Priority Tasks		:15							
		:30							
		:45							
	11	:00							
		:15							
		:30							
		:45							
	12	:00							
		:15							
		:30							
		:45							
	1	:00							
		:15							
		:30							
		:45							
	2	:00							
		:15							
		:30							
Time		:45							
	3	:00							
		:15							
		:30							
		:45							
	4	:00							
		:15							
		:30							
		:45							
	5	:00							
£		:30							
	6	:00							
		:30							
	7	:00							
		:30							
	8	:00							

Appointments

			M	T	W	T	F	S	S
Important		Appointments							
	8	:00							
		:15							
		:30							
		:45							
	9	:00							
		:15							
		:30							
		:45							
	10	:00							
Priority Tasks		:15							
		:30							
		:45							
	11	:00							
		:15							
		:30							
		:45							
	12	:00							
		:15							
		:30							
		:45							
	1	:00							
		:15							
		:30							
		:45							
	2	:00							
		:15							
		:30							
Time		:45							
	3	:00							
		:15							
		:30							
		:45							
	4	:00							
		:15							
		:30							
		:45							
	5	:00							
£		:30							
	6	:00							
		:30							
	7	:00							
		:30							
	8	:00							

Important			M	T	W	T	F	S	S
	8	:00							
		:15							
		:30							
		:45							
	9	:00							
		:15							
		:30							
		:45							
	10	:00							
Priority Tasks		:15							
		:30							
		:45							
	11	:00							
		:15							
		:30							
		:45							
	12	:00							
		:15							
		:30							
		:45							
	1	:00							
		:15							
		:30							
		:45							
	2	:00							
		:15							
		:30							
Time		:45							
	3	:00							
		:15							
		:30							
		:45							
	4	:00							
		:15							
		:30							
		:45							
	5	:00							
		:30							
£	6	:00							
		:30							
	7	:00							
		:30							
	8	:00							

Appointments

Important			Appointments						
			M	T	W	T	F	S	S
	8	:00							
		:15							
		:30							
		:45							
	9	:00							
		:15							
		:30							
		:45							
	10	:00							
Priority Tasks		:15							
		:30							
		:45							
	11	:00							
		:15							
		:30							
		:45							
	12	:00							
		:15							
		:30							
		:45							
	1	:00							
		:15							
		:30							
		:45							
	2	:00							
		:15							
		:30							
Time		:45							
	3	:00							
		:15							
		:30							
		:45							
	4	:00							
		:15							
		:30							
		:45							
	5	:00							
£		:30							
	6	:00							
		:30							
	7	:00							
		:30							
	8	:00							

Important		M	T	W	T	F	S	S
	8 :00							
	:15							
	:30							
	:45							
	9 :00							
	:15							
	:30							
	:45							
	10 :00							
Priority Tasks	:15							
	:30							
	:45							
	11 :00							
	:15							
	:30							
	:45							
	12 :00							
	:15							
	:30							
	:45							
	1 :00							
	:15							
	:30							
	:45							
	2 :00							
	:15							
	:30							
Time	:45							
	3 :00							
	:15							
	:30							
	:45							
	4 :00							
	:15							
	:30							
	:45							
	5 :00							
£	:30							
	6 :00							
	:30							
	7 :00							
	:30							
	8 :00							

Appointments

Monday 21 November 16 - Sunday 27 November 16

Important			Appointments						
			M	T	W	T	F	S	S
	8	:00							
		:15							
		:30							
		:45							
	9	:00							
		:15							
		:30							
		:45							
	10	:00							
Priority Tasks		:15							
		:30							
		:45							
	11	:00							
		:15							
		:30							
		:45							
	12	:00							
		:15							
		:30							
		:45							
	1	:00							
		:15							
		:30							
		:45							
	2	:00							
		:15							
		:30							
Time		:45							
	3	:00							
		:15							
		:30							
		:45							
	4	:00							
		:15							
		:30							
		:45							
	5	:00							
£		:30							
	6	:00							
		:30							
	7	:00							
		:30							
	8	:00							

Monday 28 November 16 - Sunday 04 December 16

Important			M	T	W	T	F	S	S
	8	:00							
		:15							
		:30							
		:45							
	9	:00							
		:15							
		:30							
		:45							
	10	:00							
Priority Tasks		:15							
		:30							
		:45							
	11	:00							
		:15							
		:30							
		:45							
	12	:00							
		:15							
		:30							
		:45							
	1	:00							
		:15							
		:30							
		:45							
	2	:00							
		:15							
		:30							
Time		:45							
	3	:00							
		:15							
		:30							
		:45							
	4	:00							
		:15							
		:30							
		:45							
	5	:00							
£		:30							
	6	:00							
		:30							
	7	:00							
		:30							
	8	:00							

Appointments

Important			Appointments						
			M	T	W	T	F	S	S
	8	:00							
		:15							
		:30							
		:45							
	9	:00							
		:15							
		:30							
		:45							
	10	:00							
Priority Tasks		:15							
		:30							
		:45							
	11	:00							
		:15							
		:30							
		:45							
	12	:00							
		:15							
		:30							
		:45							
	1	:00							
		:15							
		:30							
		:45							
	2	:00							
		:15							
		:30							
Time		:45							
	3	:00							
		:15							
		:30							
		:45							
	4	:00							
		:15							
		:30							
		:45							
	5	:00							
£		:30							
	6	:00							
		:30							
	7	:00							
		:30							
	8	:00							

Important			Appointments						
			M	T	W	T	F	S	S
	8	:00							
		:15							
		:30							
		:45							
	9	:00							
		:15							
		:30							
		:45							
	10	:00							
Priority Tasks		:15							
		:30							
		:45							
	11	:00							
		:15							
		:30							
		:45							
	12	:00							
		:15							
		:30							
		:45							
	1	:00							
		:15							
		:30							
		:45							
	2	:00							
		:15							
		:30							
Time		:45							
	3	:00							
		:15							
		:30							
		:45							
	4	:00							
		:15							
		:30							
		:45							
	5	:00							
£		:30							
	6	:00							
		:30							
	7	:00							
		:30							
	8	:00							

Important			M	T	W	T	F	S	S
	8	:00							
		:15							
		:30							
		:45							
	9	:00							
		:15							
		:30							
		:45							
	10	:00							
Priority Tasks		:15							
		:30							
		:45							
	11	:00							
		:15							
		:30							
		:45							
	12	:00							
		:15							
		:30							
		:45							
	1	:00							
		:15							
		:30							
		:45							
	2	:00							
		:15							
		:30							
Time		:45							
	3	:00							
		:15							
		:30							
		:45							
	4	:00							
		:15							
		:30							
		:45							
	5	:00							
£		:30							
	6	:00							
		:30							
	7	:00							
		:30							
	8	:00							

Appointments

Monday 26 December 16 - Sunday 1st January 2017

		Appointments						
Important		**M**	**T**	**W**	**T**	**F**	**S**	**S**
	8 :00							
	:15							
	:30							
	:45							
	9 :00							
	:15							
	:30							
	:45							
	10 :00							
Priority Tasks	:15							
	:30							
	:45							
	11 :00							
	:15							
	:30							
	:45							
	12 :00							
	:15							
	:30							
	:45							
	1 :00							
	:15							
	:30							
	:45							
	2 :00							
	:15							
	:30							
Time	:45							
	3 :00							
	:15							
	:30							
	:45							
	4 :00							
	:15							
	:30							
	:45							
	5 :00							
£	:30							
	6 :00							
	:30							
	7 :00							
	:30							
	8 :00							

01/01	FRI	Catterick Bridge (Afternoon)
01/01	FRI	Cheltenham (Afternoon)
01/01	FRI	Exeter (Afternoon)
01/01	FRI	Musselburgh (Afternoon)
01/01	FRI	Fakenham (Afternoon)
01/01	FRI	SOUTHWELL (AWT) (Afternoon)
02/01	SAT	Ayr (Afternoon)
02/01	SAT	Sandown Park (Afternoon)
02/01	SAT	SOUTHWELL (AWT) (Afternoon)
02/01	SAT	CHELMSFORD CITY (AWT) (Afternoon)
03/01	SUN	Plumpton (Afternoon)
03/01	SUN	CHELMSFORD CITY (AWT) (Afternoon)
04/01	MON	Musselburgh (Afternoon)
04/01	MON	Ludlow (Afternoon)
04/01	MON	WOLVERHAMPTON (AWT) (Afternoon)
05/01	TUE	Bangor-On-Dee (Afternoon)
05/01	TUE	LINGFIELD PARK (AWT) (Afternoon)
05/01	TUE	SOUTHWELL (AWT) (Afternoon)
06/01	WED	Huntingdon (Afternoon)
06/01	WED	KEMPTON PARK (AWT) (Twilight)
06/01	WED	WOLVERHAMPTON (AWT) (Afternoon)
06/01	WED	CHELMSFORD CITY (AWT) (Afternoon)
07/01	THU	LINGFIELD PARK (AWT) (Afternoon)
07/01	THU	Newcastle (Afternoon)
07/01	THU	Towcester (Afternoon)
07/01	THU	CHELMSFORD CITY (AWT) (Twilight)
08/01	FRI	Chepstow (Afternoon)
08/01	FRI	LINGFIELD PARK (AWT) (Afternoon)
08/01	FRI	Wetherby (Afternoon)
08/01	FRI	WOLVERHAMPTON (AWT) (Twilight)
09/01	SAT	Doncaster (Afternoon)
09/01	SAT	Kempton Park (Afternoon)
09/01	SAT	LINGFIELD PARK (AWT) (Afternoon)
09/01	SAT	Wincanton (Afternoon)
10/01	SUN	SOUTHWELL (AWT) (Afternoon)
10/01	SUN	Ffos Las (Afternoon)
11/01	MON	Ayr (Afternoon)
11/01	MON	KEMPTON PARK (AWT) (Afternoon)
11/01	MON	WOLVERHAMPTON (AWT) (Afternoon)
12/01	TUE	Fakenham (Afternoon)
12/01	TUE	LINGFIELD PARK (AWT) (Afternoon)
12/01	TUE	Ludlow (Afternoon)

13/01	WED	KEMPTON PARK (AWT) (Twilight)
13/01	WED	Newcastle (Afternoon)
13/01	WED	Taunton (Afternoon)
13/01	WED	CHELMSFORD CITY (AWT) (Afternoon)
14/01	THU	Catterick Bridge (Afternoon)
14/01	THU	Leicester (Afternoon)
14/01	THU	SOUTHWELL (AWT) (Afternoon)
14/01	THU	CHELMSFORD CITY (AWT) (Twilight)
15/01	FRI	Huntingdon (Afternoon)
15/01	FRI	LINGFIELD PARK (AWT) (Afternoon)
15/01	FRI	Sedgefield (Afternoon)
15/01	FRI	WOLVERHAMPTON (AWT) (Twilight)
16/01	SAT	LINGFIELD PARK (AWT) (Afternoon)
16/01	SAT	Warwick (Afternoon)
16/01	SAT	Wetherby (Afternoon)
16/01	SAT	CHELMSFORD CITY (AWT) (Afternoon)
17/01	SUN	Kelso (Afternoon)
17/01	SUN	KEMPTON PARK (AWT) (Afternoon)
18/01	MON	Plumpton (Afternoon)
18/01	MON	WOLVERHAMPTON (AWT) (Afternoon)
18/01	MON	Ffos Las (Afternoon)
19/01	TUE	Ayr (Afternoon)
19/01	TUE	Exeter (Afternoon)
19/01	TUE	SOUTHWELL (AWT) (Afternoon)
20/01	WED	Musselburgh (Afternoon)
20/01	WED	KEMPTON PARK (AWT) (Twilight)
20/01	WED	LINGFIELD PARK (AWT) (Afternoon)
20/01	WED	Newbury (Afternoon)
21/01	THU	Ludlow (Afternoon)
21/01	THU	SOUTHWELL (AWT) (Afternoon)
21/01	THU	Wincanton (Afternoon)
21/01	THU	CHELMSFORD CITY (AWT) (Twilight)
22/01	FRI	Chepstow (Afternoon)
22/01	FRI	LINGFIELD PARK (AWT) (Afternoon)
22/01	FRI	Market Rasen (Afternoon)
22/01	FRI	WOLVERHAMPTON (AWT) (Twilight)
23/01	SAT	Ascot (Afternoon)
23/01	SAT	Haydock Park (Afternoon)
23/01	SAT	LINGFIELD PARK (AWT) (Afternoon)
23/01	SAT	Taunton (Afternoon)
24/01	SUN	Fontwell Park (Afternoon)
24/01	SUN	CHELMSFORD CITY (AWT) (Afternoon)
25/01	MON	Kempton Park (Afternoon)
25/01	MON	Newcastle (Afternoon)
25/01	MON	WOLVERHAMPTON (AWT) (Afternoon)
26/01	TUE	Leicester (Afternoon)
26/01	TUE	SOUTHWELL (AWT) (Afternoon)

26/01	TUE	Wetherby (Afternoon)
27/01	WED	Bangor-On-Dee (Afternoon)
27/01	WED	Catterick Bridge (Afternoon)
27/01	WED	KEMPTON PARK (AWT) (Twilight)
27/01	WED	LINGFIELD PARK (AWT) (Afternoon)
28/01	THU	Fakenham (Afternoon)
28/01	THU	SOUTHWELL (AWT) (Afternoon)
28/01	THU	Warwick (Afternoon)
28/01	THU	CHELMSFORD CITY (AWT) (Twilight)
29/01	FRI	Doncaster (Afternoon)
29/01	FRI	Huntingdon (Afternoon)
29/01	FRI	LINGFIELD PARK (AWT) (Afternoon)
29/01	FRI	WOLVERHAMPTON (AWT) (Twilight)
30/01	SAT	Cheltenham (Afternoon)
30/01	SAT	Doncaster (Afternoon)
30/01	SAT	LINGFIELD PARK (AWT) (Afternoon)
30/01	SAT	Uttoxeter (Afternoon)
31/01	SUN	Fontwell Park (Afternoon)
31/01	SUN	Sedgefield (Afternoon)
01/02	MON	Ayr (Afternoon)
01/02	MON	Plumpton (Afternoon)
01/02	MON	WOLVERHAMPTON (AWT) (Afternoon)
02/02	TUE	Lingfield Park (Afternoon)
02/02	TUE	SOUTHWELL (AWT) (Afternoon)
02/02	TUE	Taunton (Afternoon)
03/02	WED	KEMPTON PARK (AWT) (Twilight)
03/02	WED	Leicester (Afternoon)
03/02	WED	Ludlow (Afternoon)
03/02	WED	Newcastle (Afternoon)
04/02	THU	SOUTHWELL (AWT) (Afternoon)
04/02	THU	Towcester (Afternoon)
04/02	THU	Wincanton (Afternoon)
04/02	THU	CHELMSFORD CITY (AWT) (Twilight)
05/02	FRI	Catterick Bridge (Afternoon)
05/02	FRI	Chepstow (Afternoon)
05/02	FRI	LINGFIELD PARK (AWT) (Afternoon)
05/02	FRI	WOLVERHAMPTON (AWT) (Twilight)
06/02	SAT	LINGFIELD PARK (AWT) (Afternoon)
06/02	SAT	Sandown Park (Afternoon)
06/02	SAT	Wetherby (Afternoon)
06/02	SAT	Ffos Las (Afternoon)
07/02	SUN	Musselburgh (Afternoon)
07/02	SUN	CHELMSFORD CITY (AWT) (Afternoon)
08/02	MON	Musselburgh (Afternoon)
08/02	MON	Fakenham (Afternoon)
08/02	MON	WOLVERHAMPTON (AWT) (Afternoon)
09/02	TUE	Market Rasen (Afternoon)

09/02	TUE	Sedgefield (Afternoon)
09/02	TUE	SOUTHWELL (AWT) (Afternoon)
10/02	WED	Carlisle (Afternoon)
10/02	WED	KEMPTON PARK (AWT) (Twilight)
10/02	WED	Ludlow (Afternoon)
10/02	WED	SOUTHWELL (AWT) (Afternoon)
11/02	THU	Doncaster (Afternoon)
11/02	THU	Huntingdon (Afternoon)
11/02	THU	Taunton (Afternoon)
11/02	THU	CHELMSFORD CITY (AWT) (Twilight)
12/02	FRI	Bangor-On-Dee (Afternoon)
12/02	FRI	Kempton Park (Afternoon)
12/02	FRI	Wetherby (Afternoon)
12/02	FRI	WOLVERHAMPTON (AWT) (Twilight)
13/02	SAT	LINGFIELD PARK (AWT) (Afternoon)
13/02	SAT	Newbury (Afternoon)
13/02	SAT	Uttoxeter (Afternoon)
13/02	SAT	Warwick (Afternoon)
13/02	SAT	WOLVERHAMPTON (AWT) (Evening)
14/02	SUN	Exeter (Afternoon)
14/02	SUN	SOUTHWELL (AWT) (Afternoon)
15/02	MON	Catterick Bridge (Afternoon)
15/02	MON	Plumpton (Afternoon)
15/02	MON	WOLVERHAMPTON (AWT) (Afternoon)
16/02	TUE	Ayr (Afternoon)
16/02	TUE	Lingfield Park (Afternoon)
16/02	TUE	SOUTHWELL (AWT) (Afternoon)
17/02	WED	Musselburgh (Afternoon)
17/02	WED	KEMPTON PARK (AWT) (Twilight)
17/02	WED	LINGFIELD PARK (AWT) (Afternoon)
17/02	WED	Towcester (Afternoon)
18/02	THU	Fontwell Park (Afternoon)
18/02	THU	Kelso (Afternoon)
18/02	THU	Leicester (Afternoon)
18/02	THU	CHELMSFORD CITY (AWT) (Twilight)
19/02	FRI	Fakenham (Afternoon)
19/02	FRI	LINGFIELD PARK (AWT) (Afternoon)
19/02	FRI	Sandown Park (Afternoon)
19/02	FRI	WOLVERHAMPTON (AWT) (Twilight)
20/02	SAT	Ascot (Afternoon)
20/02	SAT	Haydock Park (Afternoon)
20/02	SAT	LINGFIELD PARK (AWT) (Afternoon)
20/02	SAT	Wincanton (Afternoon)
21/02	SUN	Market Rasen (Afternoon)
21/02	SUN	Ffos Las (Afternoon)
22/02	MON	Carlisle (Afternoon)
22/02	MON	Lingfield Park (Afternoon)

22/02	MON	WOLVERHAMPTON (AWT) (Afternoon)
23/02	TUE	Taunton (Afternoon)
23/02	TUE	Wetherby (Afternoon)
23/02	TUE	WOLVERHAMPTON (AWT) (Afternoon)
24/02	WED	Doncaster (Afternoon)
24/02	WED	KEMPTON PARK (AWT) (Twilight)
24/02	WED	LINGFIELD PARK (AWT) (Afternoon)
24/02	WED	Ludlow (Afternoon)
25/02	THU	Huntingdon (Afternoon)
25/02	THU	LINGFIELD PARK (AWT) (Afternoon)
25/02	THU	Sedgefield (Afternoon)
25/02	THU	CHELMSFORD CITY (AWT) (Twilight)
26/02	FRI	Exeter (Afternoon)
26/02	FRI	LINGFIELD PARK (AWT) (Afternoon)
26/02	FRI	Warwick (Afternoon)
26/02	FRI	WOLVERHAMPTON (AWT) (Twilight)
27/02	SAT	Chepstow (Afternoon)
27/02	SAT	Kempton Park (Afternoon)
27/02	SAT	LINGFIELD PARK (AWT) (Afternoon)
27/02	SAT	Newcastle (Afternoon)
28/02	SUN	Fontwell Park (Afternoon)
28/02	SUN	Southwell (Afternoon)
29/02	MON	Ayr (Afternoon)
29/02	MON	Plumpton (Afternoon)
29/02	MON	WOLVERHAMPTON (AWT) (Afternoon)
01/03	TUE	Catterick Bridge (Afternoon)
01/03	TUE	Leicester (Afternoon)
01/03	TUE	LINGFIELD PARK (AWT) (Afternoon)
02/03	WED	Bangor-On-Dee (Afternoon)
02/03	WED	KEMPTON PARK (AWT) (Twilight)
02/03	WED	Wincanton (Afternoon)
02/03	WED	WOLVERHAMPTON (AWT) (Afternoon)
03/03	THU	Ludlow (Afternoon)
03/03	THU	SOUTHWELL (AWT) (Afternoon)
03/03	THU	Taunton (Afternoon)
03/03	THU	CHELMSFORD CITY (AWT) (Twilight)
04/03	FRI	Doncaster (Afternoon)
04/03	FRI	LINGFIELD PARK (AWT) (Afternoon)
04/03	FRI	Newbury (Afternoon)
04/03	FRI	WOLVERHAMPTON (AWT) (Twilight)
05/03	SAT	Doncaster (Afternoon)
05/03	SAT	Kelso (Afternoon)
05/03	SAT	LINGFIELD PARK (AWT) (Afternoon)
05/03	SAT	Newbury (Afternoon)
05/03	SAT	Stratford-On-Avon (Afternoon)
06/03	SUN	Huntingdon (Afternoon)
06/03	SUN	Sedgefield (Afternoon)

07/03	MON	Lingfield Park (Afternoon)
07/03	MON	Southwell (Afternoon)
07/03	MON	WOLVERHAMPTON (AWT) (Afternoon)
08/03	TUE	Exeter (Afternoon)
08/03	TUE	Newcastle (Afternoon)
08/03	TUE	SOUTHWELL (AWT) (Afternoon)
09/03	WED	Catterick Bridge (Afternoon)
09/03	WED	Fontwell Park (Afternoon)
09/03	WED	KEMPTON PARK (AWT) (Twilight)
09/03	WED	LINGFIELD PARK (AWT) (Afternoon)
10/03	THU	Carlisle (Afternoon)
10/03	THU	SOUTHWELL (AWT) (Afternoon)
10/03	THU	Wincanton (Afternoon)
10/03	THU	CHELMSFORD CITY (AWT) (Twilight)
11/03	FRI	Ayr (Afternoon)
11/03	FRI	Leicester (Afternoon)
11/03	FRI	Sandown Park (Afternoon)
11/03	FRI	CHELMSFORD CITY (AWT) (Twilight)
12/03	SAT	Ayr (Afternoon)
12/03	SAT	Chepstow (Afternoon)
12/03	SAT	Sandown Park (Afternoon)
12/03	SAT	WOLVERHAMPTON (AWT) (Afternoon)
13/03	SUN	Market Rasen (Afternoon)
13/03	SUN	Warwick (Afternoon)
14/03	MON	Plumpton (Afternoon)
14/03	MON	Stratford-On-Avon (Afternoon)
14/03	MON	Taunton (Afternoon)
15/03	TUE	Cheltenham (Afternoon)
15/03	TUE	Sedgefield (Afternoon)
15/03	TUE	SOUTHWELL (AWT) (Afternoon)
15/03	TUE	WOLVERHAMPTON (AWT) (Twilight)
16/03	WED	Cheltenham (Afternoon)
16/03	WED	Huntingdon (Afternoon)
16/03	WED	KEMPTON PARK (AWT) (Twilight)
16/03	WED	SOUTHWELL (AWT) (Afternoon)
17/03	THU	Cheltenham (Afternoon)
17/03	THU	Hexham (Afternoon)
17/03	THU	Towcester (Afternoon)
17/03	THU	CHELMSFORD CITY (AWT) (Twilight)
18/03	FRI	Cheltenham (Afternoon)
18/03	FRI	Fakenham (Afternoon)
18/03	FRI	LINGFIELD PARK (AWT) (Afternoon)
18/03	FRI	WOLVERHAMPTON (AWT) (Twilight)
19/03	SAT	Fontwell Park (Afternoon)
19/03	SAT	Kempton Park (Afternoon)
19/03	SAT	Newcastle (Afternoon)
19/03	SAT	Uttoxeter (Afternoon)

19/03	SAT	WOLVERHAMPTON (AWT)	(Evening)
20/03	SUN	Carlisle	(Afternoon)
20/03	SUN	Ffos Las	(Afternoon)
21/03	MON	Kelso	(Afternoon)
21/03	MON	Southwell	(Afternoon)
21/03	MON	Taunton	(Afternoon)
22/03	TUE	Exeter	(Afternoon)
22/03	TUE	SOUTHWELL (AWT)	(Afternoon)
22/03	TUE	Wetherby	(Afternoon)
23/03	WED	Haydock Park	(Afternoon)
23/03	WED	KEMPTON PARK (AWT)	(Twilight)
23/03	WED	SOUTHWELL (AWT)	(Afternoon)
23/03	WED	Warwick	(Afternoon)
24/03	THU	Chepstow	(Afternoon)
24/03	THU	Ludlow	(Afternoon)
24/03	THU	WOLVERHAMPTON (AWT)	(Afternoon)
25/03	FRI	MUSSELBURGH	(Afternoon)
25/03	FRI	LINGFIELD PARK (AWT)	(Afternoon)
26/03	SAT	Carlisle	(Afternoon)
26/03	SAT	Haydock Park	(Afternoon)
26/03	SAT	KEMPTON PARK (AWT)	(Afternoon)
26/03	SAT	Newton Abbot	(Afternoon)
26/03	SAT	Stratford-On-Avon	(Afternoon)
27/03	SUN	MUSSELBURGH	(Afternoon)
27/03	SUN	Plumpton	(Afternoon)
27/03	SUN	Sedgefield	(Afternoon)
27/03	SUN	WOLVERHAMPTON (AWT)	(Afternoon)
28/03	MON	Chepstow	(Afternoon)
28/03	MON	Fakenham	(Afternoon)
28/03	MON	Huntingdon	(Afternoon)
28/03	MON	Market Rasen	(Afternoon)
28/03	MON	Plumpton	(Afternoon)
28/03	MON	REDCAR	(Afternoon)
29/03	TUE	Hexham	(Afternoon)
29/03	TUE	Southwell	(Afternoon)
29/03	TUE	WOLVERHAMPTON (AWT)	(Afternoon)
30/03	WED	Exeter	(Afternoon)
30/03	WED	KEMPTON PARK (AWT)	(Twilight)
30/03	WED	LINGFIELD PARK (AWT)	(Afternoon)
30/03	WED	SOUTHWELL (AWT)	(Afternoon)
31/03	THU	Bangor-On-Dee	(Afternoon)
31/03	THU	WOLVERHAMPTON (AWT)	(Afternoon)
31/03	THU	Ffos Las	(Afternoon)
31/03	THU	CHELMSFORD CITY (AWT)	(Twilight)
01/04	FRI	Fontwell Park	(Afternoon)
01/04	FRI	LINGFIELD PARK (AWT)	(Afternoon)
01/04	FRI	Newbury	(Afternoon)

01/04	FRI	Wetherby (Afternoon)
01/04	FRI	WOLVERHAMPTON (AWT) (Twilight)
02/04	SAT	DONCASTER (Afternoon)
02/04	SAT	Kelso (Afternoon)
02/04	SAT	KEMPTON PARK (AWT) (Afternoon)
02/04	SAT	Newbury (Afternoon)
02/04	SAT	Uttoxeter (Afternoon)
03/04	SUN	Ascot (Afternoon)
03/04	SUN	Carlisle (Afternoon)
03/04	SUN	DONCASTER (Afternoon)
04/04	MON	LINGFIELD PARK (AWT) (Afternoon)
04/04	MON	Warwick (Afternoon)
04/04	MON	Wincanton (Afternoon)
05/04	TUE	Ludlow (Afternoon)
05/04	TUE	Newton Abbot (Afternoon)
05/04	TUE	PONTEFRACT (Afternoon)
06/04	WED	CATTERICK BRIDGE (Afternoon)
06/04	WED	KEMPTON PARK (AWT) (Twilight)
06/04	WED	LINGFIELD PARK (AWT) (Afternoon)
06/04	WED	NOTTINGHAM (Afternoon)
07/04	THU	Aintree (Afternoon)
07/04	THU	SOUTHWELL (AWT) (Afternoon)
07/04	THU	Taunton (Afternoon)
07/04	THU	CHELMSFORD CITY (AWT) (Twilight)
08/04	FRI	LEICESTER (Afternoon)
08/04	FRI	Aintree (Afternoon)
08/04	FRI	Newcastle (Afternoon)
08/04	FRI	WOLVERHAMPTON (AWT) (Twilight)
09/04	SAT	Chepstow (Afternoon)
09/04	SAT	LINGFIELD PARK (AWT) (Afternoon)
09/04	SAT	Aintree (Afternoon)
09/04	SAT	Sedgefield (Afternoon)
09/04	SAT	WOLVERHAMPTON (AWT) (Evening)
10/04	SUN	Market Rasen (Afternoon)
10/04	SUN	Ffos Las (Afternoon)
11/04	MON	Kelso (Afternoon)
11/04	MON	REDCAR (Afternoon)
11/04	MON	WINDSOR (Afternoon)
12/04	TUE	Exeter (Afternoon)
12/04	TUE	NEWMARKET (Afternoon)
12/04	TUE	SOUTHWELL (AWT) (Afternoon)
13/04	WED	BEVERLEY (Afternoon)
13/04	WED	Cheltenham (Afternoon)
13/04	WED	KEMPTON PARK (AWT) (Twilight)
13/04	WED	NEWMARKET (Afternoon)
14/04	THU	Cheltenham (Afternoon)
14/04	THU	NEWMARKET (Afternoon)

14/04	THU	RIPON (Afternoon)
14/04	THU	CHELMSFORD CITY (AWT) (Twilight)
15/04	FRI	Ayr (Afternoon)
15/04	FRI	BATH (Evening)
15/04	FRI	Fontwell Park (Afternoon)
15/04	FRI	NEWBURY (Afternoon)
15/04	FRI	Southwell (Evening)
16/04	SAT	Ayr (Afternoon)
16/04	SAT	Bangor-On-Dee (Afternoon)
16/04	SAT	NEWBURY (Afternoon)
16/04	SAT	NOTTINGHAM (Evening)
16/04	SAT	THIRSK (Afternoon)
16/04	SAT	WOLVERHAMPTON (AWT) (Evening)
17/04	SUN	Stratford-On-Avon (Afternoon)
17/04	SUN	Wetherby (Afternoon)
17/04	SUN	Wincanton (Afternoon)
18/04	MON	Hexham (Afternoon)
18/04	MON	Huntingdon (Evening)
18/04	MON	Newton Abbot (Afternoon)
18/04	MON	PONTEFRACT (Afternoon)
18/04	MON	WINDSOR (Evening)
19/04	TUE	BRIGHTON (Evening)
19/04	TUE	Kempton Park (Afternoon)
19/04	TUE	Ludlow (Afternoon)
19/04	TUE	Sedgefield (Evening)
19/04	TUE	WOLVERHAMPTON (AWT) (Afternoon)
20/04	WED	CATTERICK BRIDGE (Afternoon)
20/04	WED	EPSOM DOWNS (Afternoon)
20/04	WED	LINGFIELD PARK (AWT) (Evening)
20/04	WED	Perth (Afternoon)
20/04	WED	Taunton (Evening)
21/04	THU	BEVERLEY (Afternoon)
21/04	THU	Exeter (Evening)
21/04	THU	Market Rasen (Evening)
21/04	THU	Perth (Afternoon)
21/04	THU	Warwick (Afternoon)
22/04	FRI	Chepstow (Evening)
22/04	FRI	DONCASTER (Afternoon)
22/04	FRI	Perth (Afternoon)
22/04	FRI	Plumpton (Evening)
22/04	FRI	SANDOWN PARK (Afternoon)
23/04	SAT	DONCASTER (Evening)
23/04	SAT	HAYDOCK PARK (Afternoon)
23/04	SAT	LEICESTER (Afternoon)
23/04	SAT	RIPON (Afternoon)
23/04	SAT	Sandown Park (Afternoon)
23/04	SAT	WOLVERHAMPTON (AWT) (Evening)

24/04	SUN	MUSSELBURGH (Afternoon)
24/04	SUN	THIRSK (Afternoon)
25/04	MON	AYR (Afternoon)
25/04	MON	SOUTHWELL (AWT) (Afternoon)
25/04	MON	WINDSOR (Evening)
25/04	MON	WOLVERHAMPTON (AWT) (Evening)
25/04	MON	YARMOUTH (Afternoon)
26/04	TUE	BATH (Evening)
26/04	TUE	BRIGHTON (Afternoon)
26/04	TUE	NOTTINGHAM (Afternoon)
26/04	TUE	WOLVERHAMPTON (AWT) (Evening)
26/04	TUE	YARMOUTH (Afternoon)
27/04	WED	ASCOT (Afternoon)
27/04	WED	BRIGHTON (Evening)
27/04	WED	Cheltenham (Evening)
27/04	WED	PONTEFRACT (Afternoon)
27/04	WED	WOLVERHAMPTON (AWT) (Afternoon)
28/04	THU	LINGFIELD PARK (AWT) (Afternoon)
28/04	THU	REDCAR (Afternoon)
28/04	THU	Sedgefield (Evening)
28/04	THU	Towcester (Afternoon)
28/04	THU	CHELMSFORD CITY (AWT) (Evening)
29/04	FRI	Bangor-On-Dee (Evening)
29/04	FRI	CHEPSTOW (Afternoon)
29/04	FRI	MUSSELBURGH (Afternoon)
29/04	FRI	Fontwell Park (Evening)
29/04	FRI	LINGFIELD PARK (AWT) (Afternoon)
30/04	SAT	DONCASTER (Evening)
30/04	SAT	GOODWOOD (Afternoon)
30/04	SAT	Hexham (Evening)
30/04	SAT	NEWMARKET (Afternoon)
30/04	SAT	THIRSK (Afternoon)
30/04	SAT	Uttoxeter (Afternoon)
01/05	SUN	HAMILTON PARK (Afternoon)
01/05	SUN	NEWMARKET (Afternoon)
01/05	SUN	SALISBURY (Afternoon)
02/05	MON	BATH (Afternoon)
02/05	MON	BEVERLEY (Afternoon)
02/05	MON	Kempton Park (Afternoon)
02/05	MON	Warwick (Afternoon)
02/05	MON	WINDSOR (Afternoon)
03/05	TUE	BRIGHTON (Afternoon)
03/05	TUE	CATTERICK BRIDGE (Evening)
03/05	TUE	Exeter (Evening)
03/05	TUE	Fakenham (Afternoon)
03/05	TUE	Sedgefield (Afternoon)
04/05	WED	CHESTER (Afternoon)

04/05	WED	Kelso (Afternoon)
04/05	WED	Newton Abbot (Afternoon)
04/05	WED	Wetherby (Evening)
04/05	WED	CHELMSFORD CITY (AWT) (Evening)
05/05	THU	Carlisle (Evening)
05/05	THU	CHESTER (Afternoon)
05/05	THU	Newton Abbot (Afternoon)
05/05	THU	Uttoxeter (Afternoon)
05/05	THU	Wincanton (Evening)
06/05	FRI	ASCOT (Evening)
06/05	FRI	CHESTER (Afternoon)
06/05	FRI	LINGFIELD PARK (Afternoon)
06/05	FRI	Market Rasen (Afternoon)
06/05	FRI	NOTTINGHAM (Evening)
06/05	FRI	RIPON (Evening)
07/05	SAT	ASCOT (Afternoon)
07/05	SAT	haydock park (MIXED) (Afternoon)
07/05	SAT	Hexham (Afternoon)
07/05	SAT	LINGFIELD PARK (Afternoon)
07/05	SAT	NOTTINGHAM (Afternoon)
07/05	SAT	THIRSK (Evening)
07/05	SAT	Warwick (Evening)
08/05	SUN	Ludlow (Afternoon)
08/05	SUN	Plumpton (Afternoon)
09/05	MON	BRIGHTON (Afternoon)
09/05	MON	MUSSELBURGH (Afternoon)
09/05	MON	Towcester (Evening)
09/05	MON	WINDSOR (Evening)
09/05	MON	WOLVERHAMPTON (AWT) (Afternoon)
10/05	TUE	BEVERLEY (Afternoon)
10/05	TUE	CHEPSTOW (Evening)
10/05	TUE	Sedgefield (Afternoon)
10/05	TUE	Southwell (Evening)
10/05	TUE	Wincanton (Afternoon)
11/05	WED	BATH (Evening)
11/05	WED	Perth (Evening)
11/05	WED	Worcester (Afternoon)
11/05	WED	YARMOUTH (Afternoon)
11/05	WED	YORK (Afternoon)
12/05	THU	Fontwell Park (Evening)
12/05	THU	NEWMARKET (Evening)
12/05	THU	Perth (Afternoon)
12/05	THU	SALISBURY (Afternoon)
12/05	THU	YORK (Afternoon)
13/05	FRI	HAMILTON PARK (Evening)
13/05	FRI	Aintree (Evening)
13/05	FRI	NEWBURY (Afternoon)

13/05	FRI	NEWMARKET (Afternoon)
13/05	FRI	YORK (Afternoon)
14/05	SAT	Bangor-On-Dee (Afternoon)
14/05	SAT	DONCASTER (Evening)
14/05	SAT	NEWBURY (Afternoon)
14/05	SAT	NEWMARKET (Afternoon)
14/05	SAT	THIRSK (Afternoon)
14/05	SAT	Uttoxeter (Evening)
15/05	SUN	Market Rasen (Afternoon)
15/05	SUN	RIPON (Afternoon)
15/05	SUN	Stratford-On-Avon (Afternoon)
16/05	MON	BRIGHTON (Afternoon)
16/05	MON	Kempton Park (Afternoon)
16/05	MON	LEICESTER (Evening)
16/05	MON	REDCAR (Afternoon)
16/05	MON	WINDSOR (Evening)
17/05	TUE	Huntingdon (Evening)
17/05	TUE	NEWCASTLE (AWT) (Afternoon)
17/05	TUE	NOTTINGHAM (Afternoon)
17/05	TUE	WETHERBY (Evening)
17/05	TUE	YARMOUTH (Afternoon)
18/05	WED	AYR (Afternoon)
18/05	WED	BATH (Afternoon)
18/05	WED	KEMPTON PARK (AWT) (Evening)
18/05	WED	Southwell (Evening)
18/05	WED	Warwick (Afternoon)
19/05	THU	GOODWOOD (Afternoon)
19/05	THU	LINGFIELD PARK (Afternoon)
19/05	THU	RIPON (Evening)
19/05	THU	SANDOWN PARK (Evening)
19/05	THU	Worcester (Afternoon)
20/05	FRI	CARLISLE (Afternoon)
20/05	FRI	CATTERICK BRIDGE (Evening)
20/05	FRI	GOODWOOD (Afternoon)
20/05	FRI	HAYDOCK PARK (Evening)
20/05	FRI	Stratford-On-Avon (Evening)
20/05	FRI	WOLVERHAMPTON (AWT) (Afternoon)
21/05	SAT	CHEPSTOW (Evening)
21/05	SAT	GOODWOOD (Afternoon)
21/05	SAT	HAYDOCK PARK (Afternoon)
21/05	SAT	NEWMARKET (Afternoon)
21/05	SAT	Stratford-On-Avon (Evening)
21/05	SAT	YORK (Afternoon)
22/05	SUN	Fakenham (Afternoon)
22/05	SUN	NOTTINGHAM (Afternoon)
23/05	MON	AYR (Afternoon)
23/05	MON	CARLISLE (Evening)

23/05	MON	LEICESTER (Afternoon)
23/05	MON	WINDSOR (Evening)
24/05	TUE	Hexham (Afternoon)
24/05	TUE	Southwell (Evening)
24/05	TUE	WETHERBY (Evening)
24/05	TUE	WOLVERHAMPTON (AWT) (Afternoon)
25/05	WED	HAMILTON PARK (Afternoon)
25/05	WED	KEMPTON PARK (AWT) (Evening)
25/05	WED	LINGFIELD PARK (Afternoon)
25/05	WED	Market Rasen (Afternoon)
25/05	WED	Newton Abbot (Evening)
26/05	THU	Bangor-On-Dee (Afternoon)
26/05	THU	HAYDOCK PARK (Afternoon)
26/05	THU	NEWCASTLE (AWT) (Evening)
26/05	THU	SANDOWN PARK (Evening)
26/05	THU	YARMOUTH (Afternoon)
27/05	FRI	BRIGHTON (Afternoon)
27/05	FRI	MUSSELBURGH (Evening)
27/05	FRI	HAYDOCK PARK (Afternoon)
27/05	FRI	PONTEFRACT (Evening)
27/05	FRI	Worcester (Evening)
27/05	FRI	YARMOUTH (Afternoon)
28/05	SAT	BEVERLEY (Afternoon)
28/05	SAT	Cartmel (Afternoon)
28/05	SAT	CATTERICK BRIDGE (Afternoon)
28/05	SAT	CHESTER (Afternoon)
28/05	SAT	HAYDOCK PARK (Afternoon)
28/05	SAT	SALISBURY (Evening)
28/05	SAT	Ffos Las (Evening)
29/05	SUN	Fontwell Park (Afternoon)
29/05	SUN	Kelso (Afternoon)
29/05	SUN	Uttoxeter (Afternoon)
30/05	MON	Cartmel (Afternoon)
30/05	MON	Huntingdon (Afternoon)
30/05	MON	LEICESTER (Afternoon)
30/05	MON	REDCAR (Afternoon)
30/05	MON	WINDSOR (Afternoon)
31/05	TUE	LEICESTER (Afternoon)
31/05	TUE	LINGFIELD PARK (AWT) (Evening)
31/05	TUE	REDCAR (Afternoon)
31/05	TUE	Towcester (Afternoon)
31/05	TUE	WOLVERHAMPTON (AWT) (Evening)
01/06	WED	Cartmel (Afternoon)
01/06	WED	Fontwell Park (Afternoon)
01/06	WED	NOTTINGHAM (Afternoon)
01/06	WED	RIPON (Evening)
01/06	WED	CHELMSFORD CITY (AWT) (Evening)

02/06	THU	HAMILTON PARK (Afternoon)
02/06	THU	KEMPTON PARK (AWT) (Evening)
02/06	THU	LINGFIELD PARK (Afternoon)
02/06	THU	RIPON (Afternoon)
02/06	THU	Ffos Las (Evening)
03/06	FRI	BATH (Evening)
03/06	FRI	CATTERICK BRIDGE (Afternoon)
03/06	FRI	DONCASTER (Evening)
03/06	FRI	EPSOM DOWNS (Afternoon)
03/06	FRI	GOODWOOD (Evening)
03/06	FRI	Market Rasen (Afternoon)
04/06	SAT	DONCASTER (Afternoon)
04/06	SAT	MUSSELBURGH (Afternoon)
04/06	SAT	EPSOM DOWNS (Afternoon)
04/06	SAT	Hexham (Afternoon)
04/06	SAT	LINGFIELD PARK (Evening)
04/06	SAT	NEWCASTLE (AWT) (Evening)
04/06	SAT	Worcester (Afternoon)
05/06	SUN	GOODWOOD (Afternoon)
05/06	SUN	Perth (Afternoon)
06/06	MON	AYR (Afternoon)
06/06	MON	BRIGHTON (Afternoon)
06/06	MON	PONTEFRACT (Evening)
06/06	MON	WINDSOR (Evening)
07/06	TUE	Fontwell Park (Afternoon)
07/06	TUE	LINGFIELD PARK (Evening)
07/06	TUE	SALISBURY (Afternoon)
07/06	TUE	Southwell (Evening)
08/06	WED	BEVERLEY (Afternoon)
08/06	WED	HAMILTON PARK (Evening)
08/06	WED	HAYDOCK PARK (Afternoon)
08/06	WED	KEMPTON PARK (AWT) (Evening)
08/06	WED	YARMOUTH (Afternoon)
09/06	THU	HAYDOCK PARK (Evening)
09/06	THU	NEWBURY (Afternoon)
09/06	THU	NOTTINGHAM (Afternoon)
09/06	THU	Uttoxeter (Evening)
09/06	THU	YARMOUTH (Afternoon)
10/06	FRI	CHEPSTOW (Evening)
10/06	FRI	GOODWOOD (Evening)
10/06	FRI	Aintree (Evening)
10/06	FRI	Newton Abbot (Afternoon)
10/06	FRI	SANDOWN PARK (Afternoon)
10/06	FRI	YORK (Afternoon)
11/06	SAT	BATH (Afternoon)
11/06	SAT	CHESTER (Afternoon)
11/06	SAT	MUSSELBURGH (Afternoon)

11/06	SAT	Hexham (Afternoon)
11/06	SAT	LEICESTER (Evening)
11/06	SAT	LINGFIELD PARK (Evening)
11/06	SAT	SANDOWN PARK (Afternoon)
11/06	SAT	YORK (Afternoon)
12/06	SUN	DONCASTER (Afternoon)
12/06	SUN	SALISBURY (Afternoon)
13/06	MON	CARLISLE (Afternoon)
13/06	MON	NOTTINGHAM (Evening)
13/06	MON	THIRSK (Afternoon)
13/06	MON	WINDSOR (Evening)
14/06	TUE	ASCOT (Afternoon)
14/06	TUE	BEVERLEY (Evening)
14/06	TUE	BRIGHTON (Evening)
14/06	TUE	Stratford-On-Avon (Afternoon)
14/06	TUE	THIRSK (Afternoon)
15/06	WED	ASCOT (Afternoon)
15/06	WED	HAMILTON PARK (Afternoon)
15/06	WED	RIPON (Evening)
15/06	WED	Uttoxeter (Afternoon)
15/06	WED	CHELMSFORD CITY (AWT) (Evening)
16/06	THU	ASCOT (Afternoon)
16/06	THU	LEICESTER (Evening)
16/06	THU	LINGFIELD PARK (AWT) (Evening)
16/06	THU	RIPON (Afternoon)
16/06	THU	Ffos Las (Evening)
16/06	THU	CHELMSFORD CITY (AWT) (Afternoon)
17/06	FRI	ASCOT (Afternoon)
17/06	FRI	AYR (Evening)
17/06	FRI	GOODWOOD (Evening)
17/06	FRI	Market Rasen (Afternoon)
17/06	FRI	NEWMARKET (Evening)
17/06	FRI	REDCAR (Afternoon)
18/06	SAT	ASCOT (Afternoon)
18/06	SAT	AYR (Afternoon)
18/06	SAT	HAYDOCK PARK (Evening)
18/06	SAT	LINGFIELD PARK (Evening)
18/06	SAT	NEWMARKET (Afternoon)
18/06	SAT	REDCAR (Afternoon)
19/06	SUN	Hexham (Afternoon)
19/06	SUN	PONTEFRACT (Afternoon)
19/06	SUN	Worcester (Afternoon)
20/06	MON	CHEPSTOW (Afternoon)
20/06	MON	Southwell (Afternoon)
20/06	MON	WINDSOR (Evening)
20/06	MON	WOLVERHAMPTON (AWT) (Evening)
21/06	TUE	BEVERLEY (Afternoon)

21/06	TUE	BRIGHTON (Afternoon)
21/06	TUE	LEICESTER (Evening)
21/06	TUE	Newton Abbot (Evening)
22/06	WED	BATH (Evening)
22/06	WED	CARLISLE (Afternoon)
22/06	WED	KEMPTON PARK (AWT) (Evening)
22/06	WED	SALISBURY (Afternoon)
22/06	WED	Worcester (Afternoon)
23/06	THU	HAMILTON PARK (Evening)
23/06	THU	NEWBURY (Evening)
23/06	THU	NEWCASTLE (AWT) (Afternoon)
23/06	THU	NEWMARKET (Afternoon)
23/06	THU	NOTTINGHAM (Afternoon)
24/06	FRI	Cartmel (Afternoon)
24/06	FRI	CHESTER (Evening)
24/06	FRI	DONCASTER (Afternoon)
24/06	FRI	NEWCASTLE (AWT) (Evening)
24/06	FRI	NEWMARKET (Evening)
24/06	FRI	YARMOUTH (Afternoon)
25/06	SAT	CHESTER (Afternoon)
25/06	SAT	DONCASTER (Evening)
25/06	SAT	LINGFIELD PARK (Evening)
25/06	SAT	NEWCASTLE (AWT) (Afternoon)
25/06	SAT	NEWMARKET (Afternoon)
25/06	SAT	WINDSOR (Afternoon)
26/06	SUN	Cartmel (Afternoon)
26/06	SUN	Uttoxeter (Afternoon)
26/06	SUN	WINDSOR (Afternoon)
27/06	MON	MUSSELBURGH (Evening)
27/06	MON	PONTEFRACT (Afternoon)
27/06	MON	WINDSOR (Evening)
27/06	MON	WOLVERHAMPTON (AWT) (Afternoon)
28/06	TUE	BRIGHTON (Afternoon)
28/06	TUE	CHEPSTOW (Evening)
28/06	TUE	HAMILTON PARK (Afternoon)
28/06	TUE	Stratford-On-Avon (Evening)
29/06	WED	BATH (Evening)
29/06	WED	CATTERICK BRIDGE (Afternoon)
29/06	WED	KEMPTON PARK (AWT) (Evening)
29/06	WED	Perth (Afternoon)
29/06	WED	Worcester (Afternoon)
30/06	THU	EPSOM DOWNS (Evening)
30/06	THU	HAYDOCK PARK (Afternoon)
30/06	THU	NEWBURY (Evening)
30/06	THU	Perth (Afternoon)
30/06	THU	YARMOUTH (Afternoon)
01/07	FRI	BEVERLEY (Evening)

01/07	FRI	DONCASTER (Afternoon)
01/07	FRI	HAYDOCK PARK (Evening)
01/07	FRI	Newton Abbot (Afternoon)
01/07	FRI	SANDOWN PARK (Afternoon)
02/07	SAT	BEVERLEY (Afternoon)
02/07	SAT	CARLISLE (Evening)
02/07	SAT	HAYDOCK PARK (Afternoon)
02/07	SAT	LEICESTER (Afternoon)
02/07	SAT	NOTTINGHAM (Evening)
02/07	SAT	SANDOWN PARK (Afternoon)
03/07	SUN	AYR (Afternoon)
03/07	SUN	Market Rasen (Afternoon)
04/07	MON	AYR (Afternoon)
04/07	MON	RIPON (Evening)
04/07	MON	WINDSOR (Evening)
04/07	MON	Worcester (Afternoon)
05/07	TUE	BRIGHTON (Evening)
05/07	TUE	PONTEFRACT (Afternoon)
05/07	TUE	Uttoxeter (Evening)
05/07	TUE	WOLVERHAMPTON (AWT) (Afternoon)
06/07	WED	BATH (Evening)
06/07	WED	CATTERICK BRIDGE (Afternoon)
06/07	WED	KEMPTON PARK (AWT) (Evening)
06/07	WED	LINGFIELD PARK (Afternoon)
06/07	WED	YARMOUTH (Afternoon)
07/07	THU	CARLISLE (Afternoon)
07/07	THU	DONCASTER (Afternoon)
07/07	THU	EPSOM DOWNS (Evening)
07/07	THU	NEWBURY (Evening)
07/07	THU	NEWMARKET (Afternoon)
08/07	FRI	ASCOT (Afternoon)
08/07	FRI	CHEPSTOW (Evening)
08/07	FRI	CHESTER (Evening)
08/07	FRI	MUSSELBURGH (Afternoon)
08/07	FRI	NEWMARKET (Afternoon)
08/07	FRI	YORK (Afternoon)
09/07	SAT	ASCOT (Afternoon)
09/07	SAT	CHESTER (Afternoon)
09/07	SAT	HAMILTON PARK (Evening)
09/07	SAT	NEWMARKET (Afternoon)
09/07	SAT	SALISBURY (Evening)
09/07	SAT	YORK (Afternoon)
10/07	SUN	Perth (Afternoon)
10/07	SUN	Southwell (Afternoon)
10/07	SUN	Stratford-On-Avon (Afternoon)
11/07	MON	AYR (Afternoon)
11/07	MON	WINDSOR (Evening)

11/07	MON	WOLVERHAMPTON (AWT) (Evening)
11/07	MON	CHELMSFORD CITY (AWT) (Afternoon)
12/07	TUE	BATH (Afternoon)
12/07	TUE	BEVERLEY (Afternoon)
12/07	TUE	THIRSK (Evening)
12/07	TUE	Worcester (Evening)
13/07	WED	CATTERICK BRIDGE (Afternoon)
13/07	WED	LINGFIELD PARK (Afternoon)
13/07	WED	SANDOWN PARK (Evening)
13/07	WED	Uttoxeter (Afternoon)
13/07	WED	YARMOUTH (Evening)
14/07	THU	CHEPSTOW (Afternoon)
14/07	THU	DONCASTER (Evening)
14/07	THU	EPSOM DOWNS (Evening)
14/07	THU	HAMILTON PARK (Afternoon)
14/07	THU	LEICESTER (Afternoon)
15/07	FRI	HAMILTON PARK (Evening)
15/07	FRI	HAYDOCK PARK (Afternoon)
15/07	FRI	NEWBURY (Afternoon)
15/07	FRI	NEWMARKET (Evening)
15/07	FRI	NOTTINGHAM (Afternoon)
15/07	FRI	PONTEFRACT (Evening)
16/07	SAT	Cartmel (Afternoon)
16/07	SAT	HAYDOCK PARK (Evening)
16/07	SAT	LINGFIELD PARK (Evening)
16/07	SAT	Market Rasen (Afternoon)
16/07	SAT	NEWBURY (Afternoon)
16/07	SAT	NEWMARKET (Afternoon)
16/07	SAT	RIPON (Afternoon)
17/07	SUN	Newton Abbot (Afternoon)
17/07	SUN	REDCAR (Afternoon)
17/07	SUN	Stratford-On-Avon (Afternoon)
18/07	MON	AYR (Afternoon)
18/07	MON	BEVERLEY (Evening)
18/07	MON	Cartmel (Afternoon)
18/07	MON	WINDSOR (Evening)
19/07	TUE	MUSSELBURGH (Afternoon)
19/07	TUE	NOTTINGHAM (Evening)
19/07	TUE	FFOS LAS (Afternoon)
19/07	TUE	CHELMSFORD CITY (AWT) (Evening)
20/07	WED	BATH (Afternoon)
20/07	WED	CATTERICK BRIDGE (Afternoon)
20/07	WED	LEICESTER (Evening)
20/07	WED	LINGFIELD PARK (AWT) (Afternoon)
20/07	WED	SANDOWN PARK (Evening)
21/07	THU	DONCASTER (Evening)
21/07	THU	NEWBURY (Evening)

21/07	THU	SANDOWN PARK (Afternoon)
21/07	THU	Worcester (Afternoon)
21/07	THU	YARMOUTH (Afternoon)
22/07	FRI	ASCOT (Afternoon)
22/07	FRI	CHEPSTOW (Evening)
22/07	FRI	NEWMARKET (Evening)
22/07	FRI	THIRSK (Afternoon)
22/07	FRI	Uttoxeter (Afternoon)
22/07	FRI	YORK (Evening)
23/07	SAT	ASCOT (Afternoon)
23/07	SAT	CHESTER (Afternoon)
23/07	SAT	LINGFIELD PARK (Evening)
23/07	SAT	NEWCASTLE (AWT) (Afternoon)
23/07	SAT	NEWMARKET (Afternoon)
23/07	SAT	SALISBURY (Evening)
23/07	SAT	YORK (Afternoon)
24/07	SUN	CARLISLE (Afternoon)
24/07	SUN	PONTEFRACT (Afternoon)
24/07	SUN	Uttoxeter (Afternoon)
25/07	MON	AYR (Afternoon)
25/07	MON	Newton Abbot (Afternoon)
25/07	MON	WINDSOR (Evening)
25/07	MON	WOLVERHAMPTON (AWT) (Evening)
26/07	TUE	BEVERLEY (Afternoon)
26/07	TUE	GOODWOOD (Afternoon)
26/07	TUE	Perth (Evening)
26/07	TUE	Worcester (Evening)
26/07	TUE	YARMOUTH (Afternoon)
27/07	WED	GOODWOOD (Afternoon)
27/07	WED	LEICESTER (Evening)
27/07	WED	Perth (Afternoon)
27/07	WED	REDCAR (Afternoon)
27/07	WED	SANDOWN PARK (Evening)
28/07	THU	EPSOM DOWNS (Evening)
28/07	THU	GOODWOOD (Afternoon)
28/07	THU	NOTTINGHAM (Afternoon)
28/07	THU	Stratford-On-Avon (Afternoon)
28/07	THU	FFOS LAS (Evening)
29/07	FRI	Bangor-On-Dee (Afternoon)
29/07	FRI	BATH (Evening)
29/07	FRI	MUSSELBURGH (Evening)
29/07	FRI	GOODWOOD (Afternoon)
29/07	FRI	NEWMARKET (Evening)
29/07	FRI	THIRSK (Afternoon)
30/07	SAT	DONCASTER (Afternoon)
30/07	SAT	GOODWOOD (Afternoon)
30/07	SAT	HAMILTON PARK (Evening)

30/07	SAT	LINGFIELD PARK (Evening)
30/07	SAT	NEWMARKET (Afternoon)
30/07	SAT	THIRSK (Afternoon)
31/07	SUN	CHEPSTOW (Afternoon)
31/07	SUN	CHESTER (Afternoon)
31/07	SUN	Market Rasen (Afternoon)
01/08	MON	CARLISLE (Evening)
01/08	MON	KEMPTON PARK (AWT) (Afternoon)
01/08	MON	RIPON (Afternoon)
01/08	MON	WINDSOR (Evening)
02/08	TUE	CATTERICK BRIDGE (Afternoon)
02/08	TUE	NOTTINGHAM (Evening)
02/08	TUE	SALISBURY (Afternoon)
02/08	TUE	CHELMSFORD CITY (AWT) (Evening)
03/08	WED	BATH (Afternoon)
03/08	WED	BRIGHTON (Afternoon)
03/08	WED	KEMPTON PARK (AWT) (Evening)
03/08	WED	PONTEFRACT (Afternoon)
03/08	WED	YARMOUTH (Evening)
04/08	THU	BRIGHTON (Afternoon)
04/08	THU	HAYDOCK PARK (Afternoon)
04/08	THU	NEWCASTLE (AWT) (Evening)
04/08	THU	SANDOWN PARK (Evening)
04/08	THU	WOLVERHAMPTON (AWT) (Evening)
04/08	THU	YARMOUTH (Afternoon)
05/08	FRI	BRIGHTON (Afternoon)
05/08	FRI	MUSSELBURGH (Afternoon)
05/08	FRI	HAYDOCK PARK (Evening)
05/08	FRI	NEWMARKET (Evening)
05/08	FRI	WOLVERHAMPTON (AWT) (Afternoon)
06/08	SAT	ASCOT (Afternoon)
06/08	SAT	AYR (Evening)
06/08	SAT	HAYDOCK PARK (Afternoon)
06/08	SAT	LINGFIELD PARK (Evening)
06/08	SAT	NEWMARKET (Afternoon)
06/08	SAT	REDCAR (Afternoon)
07/08	SUN	LEICESTER (Afternoon)
07/08	SUN	WINDSOR (Afternoon)
07/08	SUN	CHELMSFORD CITY (AWT) (Afternoon)
08/08	MON	AYR (Afternoon)
08/08	MON	FFOS LAS (Evening)
08/08	MON	WINDSOR (Evening)
08/08	MON	WOLVERHAMPTON (AWT) (Afternoon)
09/08	TUE	CHEPSTOW (Afternoon)
09/08	TUE	LINGFIELD PARK (Evening)
09/08	TUE	NOTTINGHAM (Evening)
09/08	TUE	THIRSK (Afternoon)

10/08	WED	BATH (Evening)
10/08	WED	BEVERLEY (Afternoon)
10/08	WED	KEMPTON PARK (AWT) (Evening)
10/08	WED	Newton Abbot (Afternoon)
10/08	WED	SALISBURY (Afternoon)
11/08	THU	BEVERLEY (Afternoon)
11/08	THU	SALISBURY (Afternoon)
11/08	THU	Worcester (Afternoon)
11/08	THU	YARMOUTH (Evening)
11/08	THU	Stratford-On-Avon (Evening)
12/08	FRI	CATTERICK BRIDGE (Evening)
12/08	FRI	NEWBURY (Afternoon)
12/08	FRI	NEWCASTLE (AWT) (Afternoon)
12/08	FRI	NEWMARKET (Evening)
12/08	FRI	NOTTINGHAM (Afternoon)
13/08	SAT	DONCASTER (Afternoon)
13/08	SAT	LINGFIELD PARK (Evening)
13/08	SAT	Market Rasen (Evening)
13/08	SAT	NEWBURY (Afternoon)
13/08	SAT	NEWMARKET (Afternoon)
13/08	SAT	RIPON (Afternoon)
14/08	SUN	PONTEFRACT (Afternoon)
14/08	SUN	Southwell (Afternoon)
15/08	MON	AYR (Evening)
15/08	MON	THIRSK (Afternoon)
15/08	MON	WINDSOR (Evening)
15/08	MON	CHELMSFORD CITY (AWT) (Afternoon)
16/08	TUE	KEMPTON PARK (AWT) (Afternoon)
16/08	TUE	LEICESTER (Evening)
16/08	TUE	RIPON (Afternoon)
16/08	TUE	WOLVERHAMPTON (AWT) (Evening)
17/08	WED	CARLISLE (Afternoon)
17/08	WED	CHEPSTOW (Afternoon)
17/08	WED	KEMPTON PARK (AWT) (Evening)
17/08	WED	Worcester (Evening)
17/08	WED	YORK (Afternoon)
18/08	THU	CHEPSTOW (Afternoon)
18/08	THU	Fontwell Park (Evening)
18/08	THU	HAMILTON PARK (Evening)
18/08	THU	Stratford-On-Avon (Afternoon)
18/08	THU	YORK (Afternoon)
19/08	FRI	Bangor-On-Dee (Afternoon)
19/08	FRI	SALISBURY (Evening)
19/08	FRI	SANDOWN PARK (Afternoon)
19/08	FRI	WOLVERHAMPTON (AWT) (Evening)
19/08	FRI	YORK (Afternoon)
20/08	SAT	BATH (Evening)

20/08	SAT	CHESTER (Afternoon)
20/08	SAT	Newton Abbot (Afternoon)
20/08	SAT	Perth (Afternoon)
20/08	SAT	SANDOWN PARK (Afternoon)
20/08	SAT	YORK (Afternoon)
20/08	SAT	CHELMSFORD CITY (AWT) (Evening)
21/08	SUN	BRIGHTON (Afternoon)
21/08	SUN	Worcester (Afternoon)
21/08	SUN	CHELMSFORD CITY (AWT) (Afternoon)
22/08	MON	BRIGHTON (Afternoon)
22/08	MON	CARLISLE (Afternoon)
22/08	MON	KEMPTON PARK (AWT) (Evening)
22/08	MON	THIRSK (Evening)
23/08	TUE	NEWBURY (Evening)
23/08	TUE	Southwell (Afternoon)
23/08	TUE	YARMOUTH (Afternoon)
23/08	TUE	CHELMSFORD CITY (AWT) (Evening)
24/08	WED	CATTERICK BRIDGE (Afternoon)
24/08	WED	MUSSELBURGH (Afternoon)
24/08	WED	KEMPTON PARK (AWT) (Evening)
24/08	WED	LINGFIELD PARK (Afternoon)
24/08	WED	Stratford-On-Avon (Evening)
25/08	THU	MUSSELBURGH (Afternoon)
25/08	THU	Fontwell Park (Afternoon)
25/08	THU	LEICESTER (Afternoon)
25/08	THU	Sedgefield (Evening)
25/08	THU	WOLVERHAMPTON (AWT) (Evening)
26/08	FRI	GOODWOOD (Evening)
26/08	FRI	HAMILTON PARK (Evening)
26/08	FRI	NEWCASTLE (AWT) (Evening)
26/08	FRI	NEWMARKET (Afternoon)
26/08	FRI	THIRSK (Afternoon)
26/08	FRI	FFOS LAS (Afternoon)
27/08	SAT	BEVERLEY (Afternoon)
27/08	SAT	Cartmel (Afternoon)
27/08	SAT	GOODWOOD (Afternoon)
27/08	SAT	NEWMARKET (Afternoon)
27/08	SAT	REDCAR (Evening)
27/08	SAT	WINDSOR (Evening)
28/08	SUN	BEVERLEY (Afternoon)
28/08	SUN	GOODWOOD (Afternoon)
28/08	SUN	YARMOUTH (Afternoon)
29/08	MON	Cartmel (Afternoon)
29/08	MON	CHEPSTOW (Afternoon)
29/08	MON	EPSOM DOWNS (Afternoon)
29/08	MON	NEWCASTLE (AWT) (Afternoon)
29/08	MON	RIPON (Afternoon)

30/08	TUE	EPSOM DOWNS (Afternoon)
30/08	TUE	GOODWOOD (Afternoon)
30/08	TUE	HAMILTON PARK (Afternoon)
30/08	TUE	RIPON (Evening)
30/08	TUE	Worcester (Evening)
31/08	WED	BATH (Afternoon)
31/08	WED	CARLISLE (Evening)
31/08	WED	LINGFIELD PARK (Afternoon)
31/08	WED	Newton Abbot (Evening)
31/08	WED	Southwell (Afternoon)
01/09	THU	HAYDOCK PARK (Afternoon)
01/09	THU	SALISBURY (Afternoon)
01/09	THU	Sedgefield (Afternoon)
01/09	THU	CHELMSFORD CITY (AWT) (Twilight)
02/09	FRI	ASCOT (Afternoon)
02/09	FRI	MUSSELBURGH (Twilight)
02/09	FRI	HAYDOCK PARK (Afternoon)
02/09	FRI	KEMPTON PARK (AWT) (Evening)
02/09	FRI	NEWCASTLE (AWT) (Afternoon)
03/09	SAT	ASCOT (Afternoon)
03/09	SAT	HAYDOCK PARK (Afternoon)
03/09	SAT	KEMPTON PARK (AWT) (Afternoon)
03/09	SAT	Stratford-On-Avon (Afternoon)
03/09	SAT	THIRSK (Afternoon)
03/09	SAT	WOLVERHAMPTON (AWT) (Evening)
04/09	SUN	Fontwell Park (Afternoon)
04/09	SUN	YORK (Afternoon)
05/09	MON	BRIGHTON (Afternoon)
05/09	MON	Perth (Afternoon)
05/09	MON	WINDSOR (Afternoon)
06/09	TUE	LEICESTER (Afternoon)
06/09	TUE	Perth (Twilight)
06/09	TUE	REDCAR (Afternoon)
06/09	TUE	Worcester (Afternoon)
07/09	WED	CARLISLE (Afternoon)
07/09	WED	DONCASTER (Afternoon)
07/09	WED	KEMPTON PARK (AWT) (Twilight)
07/09	WED	Uttoxeter (Afternoon)
08/09	THU	CHEPSTOW (Afternoon)
08/09	THU	DONCASTER (Afternoon)
08/09	THU	EPSOM DOWNS (Afternoon)
08/09	THU	CHELMSFORD CITY (AWT) (Twilight)
09/09	FRI	CHESTER (Afternoon)
09/09	FRI	DONCASTER (Afternoon)
09/09	FRI	SALISBURY (Twilight)
09/09	FRI	SANDOWN PARK (Afternoon)
10/09	SAT	BATH (Afternoon)

10/09	SAT	CHESTER (Afternoon)
10/09	SAT	DONCASTER (Afternoon)
10/09	SAT	MUSSELBURGH (Twilight)
10/09	SAT	LINGFIELD PARK (Afternoon)
11/09	SUN	BATH (Afternoon)
11/09	SUN	FFOS LAS (Afternoon)
11/09	SUN	CHELMSFORD CITY (AWT) (Afternoon)
12/09	MON	BRIGHTON (Afternoon)
12/09	MON	KEMPTON PARK (AWT) (Afternoon)
12/09	MON	Worcester (Afternoon)
13/09	TUE	CARLISLE (Twilight)
13/09	TUE	CHEPSTOW (Afternoon)
13/09	TUE	THIRSK (Afternoon)
13/09	TUE	YARMOUTH (Afternoon)
14/09	WED	BEVERLEY (Afternoon)
14/09	WED	Kelso (Twilight)
14/09	WED	SANDOWN PARK (Afternoon)
14/09	WED	YARMOUTH (Afternoon)
15/09	THU	AYR (Afternoon)
15/09	THU	PONTEFRACT (Afternoon)
15/09	THU	YARMOUTH (Afternoon)
15/09	THU	CHELMSFORD CITY (AWT) (Twilight)
16/09	FRI	AYR (Afternoon)
16/09	FRI	Hexham (Twilight)
16/09	FRI	NEWBURY (Afternoon)
16/09	FRI	Newton Abbot (Afternoon)
17/09	SAT	AYR (Afternoon)
17/09	SAT	CATTERICK BRIDGE (Afternoon)
17/09	SAT	NEWBURY (Afternoon)
17/09	SAT	NEWMARKET (Afternoon)
17/09	SAT	WOLVERHAMPTON (AWT) (Evening)
18/09	SUN	Plumpton (Afternoon)
18/09	SUN	Uttoxeter (Afternoon)
19/09	MON	HAMILTON PARK (Afternoon)
19/09	MON	KEMPTON PARK (AWT) (Afternoon)
19/09	MON	LEICESTER (Afternoon)
20/09	TUE	BEVERLEY (Afternoon)
20/09	TUE	LINGFIELD PARK (AWT) (Afternoon)
20/09	TUE	Warwick (Afternoon)
20/09	TUE	FFOS LAS (Twilight)
21/09	WED	GOODWOOD (Afternoon)
21/09	WED	KEMPTON PARK (AWT) (Twilight)
21/09	WED	Perth (Afternoon)
21/09	WED	REDCAR (Afternoon)
22/09	THU	NEWMARKET (Afternoon)
22/09	THU	Perth (Afternoon)
22/09	THU	PONTEFRACT (Afternoon)

22/09	THU	CHELMSFORD CITY (AWT) (Twilight)
23/09	FRI	HAYDOCK PARK (Afternoon)
23/09	FRI	NEWCASTLE (AWT) (Twilight)
23/09	FRI	NEWMARKET (Afternoon)
23/09	FRI	Worcester (Afternoon)
24/09	SAT	CHESTER (Afternoon)
24/09	SAT	HAMILTON PARK (Twilight)
24/09	SAT	HAYDOCK PARK (Afternoon)
24/09	SAT	Market Rasen (Afternoon)
24/09	SAT	NEWMARKET (Afternoon)
24/09	SAT	RIPON (Afternoon)
25/09	SUN	MUSSELBURGH (Afternoon)
25/09	SUN	EPSOM DOWNS (Afternoon)
26/09	MON	BATH (Afternoon)
26/09	MON	HAMILTON PARK (Afternoon)
26/09	MON	Newton Abbot (Afternoon)
27/09	TUE	AYR (Afternoon)
27/09	TUE	Sedgefield (Afternoon)
27/09	TUE	Southwell (Afternoon)
27/09	TUE	WOLVERHAMPTON (AWT) (Twilight)
28/09	WED	Bangor-On-Dee (Afternoon)
28/09	WED	KEMPTON PARK (AWT) (Twilight)
28/09	WED	NOTTINGHAM (Afternoon)
28/09	WED	SALISBURY (Afternoon)
29/09	THU	BRIGHTON (Afternoon)
29/09	THU	NEWCASTLE (AWT) (Afternoon)
29/09	THU	Warwick (Afternoon)
29/09	THU	CHELMSFORD CITY (AWT) (Twilight)
30/09	FRI	ASCOT (Afternoon)
30/09	FRI	Fontwell Park (Afternoon)
30/09	FRI	Hexham (Afternoon)
30/09	FRI	NEWCASTLE (AWT) (Twilight)
01/10	SAT	ASCOT (Afternoon)
01/10	SAT	Fontwell Park (Afternoon)
01/10	SAT	NEWMARKET (Afternoon)
01/10	SAT	REDCAR (Afternoon)
01/10	SAT	WOLVERHAMPTON (AWT) (Evening)
02/10	SUN	Huntingdon (Afternoon)
02/10	SUN	Kelso (Afternoon)
02/10	SUN	Uttoxeter (Afternoon)
03/10	MON	PONTEFRACT (Afternoon)
03/10	MON	Southwell (Afternoon)
03/10	MON	WINDSOR (Afternoon)
04/10	TUE	BRIGHTON (Afternoon)
04/10	TUE	CATTERICK BRIDGE (Afternoon)
04/10	TUE	KEMPTON PARK (AWT) (Twilight)
04/10	TUE	LEICESTER (Afternoon)

05/10	WED	KEMPTON PARK (AWT) (Twilight)
05/10	WED	Ludlow (Afternoon)
05/10	WED	NOTTINGHAM (Afternoon)
05/10	WED	Towcester (Afternoon)
06/10	THU	AYR (Afternoon)
06/10	THU	Exeter (Afternoon)
06/10	THU	Worcester (Afternoon)
06/10	THU	CHELMSFORD CITY (AWT) (Twilight)
07/10	FRI	NEWCASTLE (AWT) (Twilight)
07/10	FRI	NEWMARKET (Afternoon)
07/10	FRI	Newton Abbot (Afternoon)
07/10	FRI	YORK (Afternoon)
08/10	SAT	Chepstow (Afternoon)
08/10	SAT	Hexham (Afternoon)
08/10	SAT	NEWCASTLE (AWT) (Twilight)
08/10	SAT	NEWMARKET (Afternoon)
08/10	SAT	YORK (Afternoon)
09/10	SUN	Chepstow (Afternoon)
09/10	SUN	GOODWOOD (Afternoon)
10/10	MON	SALISBURY (Afternoon)
10/10	MON	WINDSOR (Afternoon)
10/10	MON	YARMOUTH (Afternoon)
11/10	TUE	MUSSELBURGH (Afternoon)
11/10	TUE	Huntingdon (Afternoon)
11/10	TUE	LEICESTER (Afternoon)
11/10	TUE	WOLVERHAMPTON (AWT) (Twilight)
12/10	WED	BATH (Afternoon)
12/10	WED	KEMPTON PARK (AWT) (Twilight)
12/10	WED	NOTTINGHAM (Afternoon)
12/10	WED	Wetherby (Afternoon)
13/10	THU	BRIGHTON (Afternoon)
13/10	THU	Carlisle (Afternoon)
13/10	THU	Uttoxeter (Afternoon)
13/10	THU	CHELMSFORD CITY (AWT) (Twilight)
14/10	FRI	Fakenham (Afternoon)
14/10	FRI	HAYDOCK PARK (Afternoon)
14/10	FRI	NEWCASTLE (AWT) (Twilight)
14/10	FRI	REDCAR (Afternoon)
14/10	FRI	Wincanton (Afternoon)
15/10	SAT	ASCOT (Afternoon)
15/10	SAT	CATTERICK BRIDGE (Afternoon)
15/10	SAT	Market Rasen (Afternoon)
15/10	SAT	Stratford-On-Avon (Afternoon)
15/10	SAT	WOLVERHAMPTON (AWT) (Evening)
15/10	SAT	Ffos Las (Afternoon)
16/10	SUN	Kempton Park (Afternoon)
16/10	SUN	NEWCASTLE (AWT) (Afternoon)

17/10	MON	Plumpton (Afternoon)
17/10	MON	PONTEFRACT (Afternoon)
17/10	MON	WINDSOR (Afternoon)
18/10	TUE	Exeter (Afternoon)
18/10	TUE	KEMPTON PARK (AWT) (Twilight)
18/10	TUE	NEWCASTLE (AWT) (Afternoon)
18/10	TUE	YARMOUTH (Afternoon)
19/10	WED	Fontwell Park (Afternoon)
19/10	WED	KEMPTON PARK (AWT) (Twilight)
19/10	WED	NEWMARKET (Afternoon)
19/10	WED	Worcester (Afternoon)
20/10	THU	Carlisle (Afternoon)
20/10	THU	Ludlow (Afternoon)
20/10	THU	Newton Abbot (Afternoon)
20/10	THU	CHELMSFORD CITY (AWT) (Twilight)
21/10	FRI	Cheltenham (Afternoon)
21/10	FRI	DONCASTER (Afternoon)
21/10	FRI	NEWBURY (Afternoon)
21/10	FRI	WOLVERHAMPTON (AWT) (Twilight)
22/10	SAT	Cheltenham (Afternoon)
22/10	SAT	DONCASTER (Afternoon)
22/10	SAT	Kelso (Afternoon)
22/10	SAT	NEWBURY (Afternoon)
22/10	SAT	CHELMSFORD CITY (AWT) (Twilight)
23/10	SUN	Aintree (Afternoon)
23/10	SUN	Wincanton (Afternoon)
24/10	MON	Ayr (Afternoon)
24/10	MON	LEICESTER (Afternoon)
24/10	MON	REDCAR (Afternoon)
25/10	TUE	Bangor-On-Dee (Afternoon)
25/10	TUE	CATTERICK BRIDGE (Afternoon)
25/10	TUE	Chepstow (Afternoon)
25/10	TUE	NEWCASTLE (AWT) (Twilight)
26/10	WED	Fakenham (Afternoon)
26/10	WED	KEMPTON PARK (AWT) (Twilight)
26/10	WED	NOTTINGHAM (Afternoon)
26/10	WED	CHELMSFORD CITY (AWT) (Afternoon)
27/10	THU	LINGFIELD PARK (AWT) (Afternoon)
27/10	THU	Sedgefield (Afternoon)
27/10	THU	Stratford-On-Avon (Afternoon)
27/10	THU	CHELMSFORD CITY (AWT) (Twilight)
28/10	FRI	NEWCASTLE (AWT) (Twilight)
28/10	FRI	NEWMARKET (Afternoon)
28/10	FRI	Uttoxeter (Afternoon)
28/10	FRI	Wetherby (Afternoon)
29/10	SAT	Ascot (Afternoon)
29/10	SAT	Ayr (Afternoon)

29/10	SAT	NEWMARKET (Afternoon)
29/10	SAT	Wetherby (Afternoon)
29/10	SAT	CHELMSFORD CITY (AWT) (Twilight)
30/10	SUN	Carlisle (Afternoon)
30/10	SUN	Huntingdon (Afternoon)
31/10	MON	KEMPTON PARK (AWT) (Afternoon)
31/10	MON	Plumpton (Afternoon)
31/10	MON	Southwell (Afternoon)
01/11	TUE	Exeter (Afternoon)
01/11	TUE	KEMPTON PARK (AWT) (Twilight)
01/11	TUE	REDCAR (Afternoon)
01/11	TUE	WOLVERHAMPTON (AWT) (Afternoon)
02/11	WED	Chepstow (Afternoon)
02/11	WED	Musselburgh (Afternoon)
02/11	WED	KEMPTON PARK (AWT) (Twilight)
02/11	WED	NOTTINGHAM (Afternoon)
03/11	THU	Musselburgh (Afternoon)
03/11	THU	Market Rasen (Afternoon)
03/11	THU	Newbury (Afternoon)
03/11	THU	CHELMSFORD CITY (AWT) (Twilight)
04/11	FRI	Fontwell Park (Afternoon)
04/11	FRI	Hexham (Afternoon)
04/11	FRI	NEWCASTLE (AWT) (Twilight)
04/11	FRI	Warwick (Afternoon)
05/11	SAT	DONCASTER (Afternoon)
05/11	SAT	Kelso (Afternoon)
05/11	SAT	Aintree (Afternoon)
05/11	SAT	Wincanton (Afternoon)
05/11	SAT	CHELMSFORD CITY (AWT) (Twilight)
06/11	SUN	Sandown Park (Afternoon)
06/11	SUN	Ffos Las (Afternoon)
07/11	MON	Carlisle (Afternoon)
07/11	MON	Kempton Park (Afternoon)
07/11	MON	NEWCASTLE (AWT) (Afternoon)
08/11	TUE	Huntingdon (Afternoon)
08/11	TUE	Lingfield Park (Afternoon)
08/11	TUE	NEWCASTLE (AWT) (Twilight)
08/11	TUE	Sedgefield (Afternoon)
09/11	WED	Ayr (Afternoon)
09/11	WED	Bangor-On-Dee (Afternoon)
09/11	WED	Exeter (Afternoon)
09/11	WED	KEMPTON PARK (AWT) (Twilight)
10/11	THU	Ludlow (Afternoon)
10/11	THU	SOUTHWELL (AWT) (Afternoon)
10/11	THU	Taunton (Afternoon)
10/11	THU	CHELMSFORD CITY (AWT) (Twilight)
11/11	FRI	Cheltenham (Afternoon)

11/11	FRI	LINGFIELD PARK (AWT) (Afternoon)
11/11	FRI	Newcastle (Afternoon)
11/11	FRI	WOLVERHAMPTON (AWT) (Twilight)
12/11	SAT	Cheltenham (Afternoon)
12/11	SAT	LINGFIELD PARK (AWT) (Afternoon)
12/11	SAT	Uttoxeter (Afternoon)
12/11	SAT	Wetherby (Afternoon)
12/11	SAT	WOLVERHAMPTON (AWT) (Evening)
13/11	SUN	Cheltenham (Afternoon)
13/11	SUN	Fontwell Park (Afternoon)
14/11	MON	Leicester (Afternoon)
14/11	MON	NEWCASTLE (AWT) (Afternoon)
14/11	MON	Plumpton (Afternoon)
15/11	TUE	Fakenham (Afternoon)
15/11	TUE	LINGFIELD PARK (AWT) (Afternoon)
15/11	TUE	Southwell (Afternoon)
16/11	WED	Chepstow (Afternoon)
16/11	WED	Hexham (Afternoon)
16/11	WED	KEMPTON PARK (AWT) (Twilight)
16/11	WED	Warwick (Afternoon)
17/11	THU	Market Rasen (Afternoon)
17/11	THU	NEWCASTLE (AWT) (Afternoon)
17/11	THU	Wincanton (Afternoon)
17/11	THU	CHELMSFORD CITY (AWT) (Twilight)
18/11	FRI	Ascot (Afternoon)
18/11	FRI	Haydock Park (Afternoon)
18/11	FRI	NEWCASTLE (AWT) (Twilight)
18/11	FRI	Ffos Las (Afternoon)
19/11	SAT	Ascot (Afternoon)
19/11	SAT	Haydock Park (Afternoon)
19/11	SAT	Huntingdon (Afternoon)
19/11	SAT	LINGFIELD PARK (AWT) (Afternoon)
19/11	SAT	WOLVERHAMPTON (AWT) (Evening)
20/11	SUN	Exeter (Afternoon)
20/11	SUN	Uttoxeter (Afternoon)
21/11	MON	Kempton Park (Afternoon)
21/11	MON	Ludlow (Afternoon)
21/11	MON	CHELMSFORD CITY (AWT) (Afternoon)
22/11	TUE	Lingfield Park (Afternoon)
22/11	TUE	Sedgefield (Afternoon)
22/11	TUE	SOUTHWELL (AWT) (Afternoon)
23/11	WED	Fontwell Park (Afternoon)
23/11	WED	KEMPTON PARK (AWT) (Twilight)
23/11	WED	Wetherby (Afternoon)
23/11	WED	WOLVERHAMPTON (AWT) (Afternoon)
24/11	THU	Musselburgh (Afternoon)
24/11	THU	Taunton (Afternoon)

24/11	THU	Towcester (Afternoon)
24/11	THU	CHELMSFORD CITY (AWT) (Twilight)
25/11	FRI	Doncaster (Afternoon)
25/11	FRI	Newbury (Afternoon)
25/11	FRI	NEWCASTLE (AWT) (Afternoon)
25/11	FRI	WOLVERHAMPTON (AWT) (Twilight)
26/11	SAT	Bangor-On-Dee (Afternoon)
26/11	SAT	Doncaster (Afternoon)
26/11	SAT	Newbury (Afternoon)
26/11	SAT	Newcastle (Afternoon)
26/11	SAT	WOLVERHAMPTON (AWT) (Evening)
27/11	SUN	Carlisle (Afternoon)
27/11	SUN	Leicester (Afternoon)
28/11	MON	Ludlow (Afternoon)
28/11	MON	NEWCASTLE (AWT) (Afternoon)
28/11	MON	Plumpton (Afternoon)
29/11	TUE	Lingfield Park (Afternoon)
29/11	TUE	NEWCASTLE (AWT) (Afternoon)
29/11	TUE	Southwell (Afternoon)
30/11	WED	Catterick Bridge (Afternoon)
30/11	WED	KEMPTON PARK (AWT) (Twilight)
30/11	WED	LINGFIELD PARK (AWT) (Afternoon)
30/11	WED	Ffos Las (Afternoon)
01/12	THU	Leicester (Afternoon)
01/12	THU	Market Rasen (Afternoon)
01/12	THU	Wincanton (Afternoon)
01/12	THU	CHELMSFORD CITY (AWT) (Twilight)
02/12	FRI	Exeter (Afternoon)
02/12	FRI	Sandown Park (Afternoon)
02/12	FRI	Sedgefield (Afternoon)
02/12	FRI	WOLVERHAMPTON (AWT) (Twilight)
03/12	SAT	Chepstow (Afternoon)
03/12	SAT	Aintree (Afternoon)
03/12	SAT	Sandown Park (Afternoon)
03/12	SAT	Wetherby (Afternoon)
03/12	SAT	WOLVERHAMPTON (AWT) (Evening)
04/12	SUN	Huntingdon (Afternoon)
04/12	SUN	Kelso (Afternoon)
05/12	MON	Ayr (Afternoon)
05/12	MON	LINGFIELD PARK (AWT) (Afternoon)
05/12	MON	Ludlow (Afternoon)
06/12	TUE	Fontwell Park (Afternoon)
06/12	TUE	SOUTHWELL (AWT) (Afternoon)
06/12	TUE	Uttoxeter (Afternoon)
07/12	WED	Hexham (Afternoon)
07/12	WED	KEMPTON PARK (AWT) (Twilight)
07/12	WED	Leicester (Afternoon)

07/12	WED	LINGFIELD PARK (AWT) (Afternoon)
08/12	THU	Newcastle (Afternoon)
08/12	THU	Taunton (Afternoon)
08/12	THU	Warwick (Afternoon)
08/12	THU	CHELMSFORD CITY (AWT) (Twilight)
09/12	FRI	Bangor-On-Dee (Afternoon)
09/12	FRI	Cheltenham (Afternoon)
09/12	FRI	Doncaster (Afternoon)
09/12	FRI	NEWCASTLE (AWT) (Twilight)
10/12	SAT	Cheltenham (Afternoon)
10/12	SAT	Doncaster (Afternoon)
10/12	SAT	Lingfield Park (Afternoon)
10/12	SAT	NEWCASTLE (AWT) (Afternoon)
10/12	SAT	WOLVERHAMPTON (AWT) (Evening)
11/12	SUN	Carlisle (Afternoon)
11/12	SUN	Southwell (Afternoon)
12/12	MON	Plumpton (Afternoon)
12/12	MON	WOLVERHAMPTON (AWT) (Afternoon)
12/12	MON	Ffos Las (Afternoon)
13/12	TUE	Catterick Bridge (Afternoon)
13/12	TUE	SOUTHWELL (AWT) (Afternoon)
13/12	TUE	Wincanton (Afternoon)
14/12	WED	Musselburgh (Afternoon)
14/12	WED	KEMPTON PARK (AWT) (Twilight)
14/12	WED	LINGFIELD PARK (AWT) (Afternoon)
14/12	WED	Newbury (Afternoon)
15/12	THU	Exeter (Afternoon)
15/12	THU	NEWCASTLE (AWT) (Afternoon)
15/12	THU	Towcester (Afternoon)
15/12	THU	CHELMSFORD CITY (AWT) (Twilight)
16/12	FRI	Ascot (Afternoon)
16/12	FRI	NEWCASTLE (AWT) (Afternoon)
16/12	FRI	Uttoxeter (Afternoon)
16/12	FRI	WOLVERHAMPTON (AWT) (Twilight)
17/12	SAT	Ascot (Afternoon)
17/12	SAT	Haydock Park (Afternoon)
17/12	SAT	LINGFIELD PARK (AWT) (Afternoon)
17/12	SAT	Newcastle (Afternoon)
18/12	SUN	Fakenham (Afternoon)
18/12	SUN	LINGFIELD PARK (AWT) (Afternoon)
19/12	MON	Ayr (Afternoon)
19/12	MON	Lingfield Park (Afternoon)
19/12	MON	CHELMSFORD CITY (AWT) (Afternoon)
20/12	TUE	KEMPTON PARK (AWT) (Afternoon)
20/12	TUE	SOUTHWELL (AWT) (Afternoon)
20/12	TUE	Taunton (Afternoon)
21/12	WED	Ludlow (Afternoon)

21/12	WED	NEWCASTLE (AWT) (Afternoon)
21/12	WED	Ffos Las (Afternoon)
22/12	THU	Bangor-On-Dee (Afternoon)
22/12	THU	WOLVERHAMPTON (AWT) (Afternoon)
22/12	THU	CHELMSFORD CITY (AWT) (Afternoon)
26/12	MON	Fontwell Park (Afternoon)
26/12	MON	Huntingdon (Afternoon)
26/12	MON	Kempton Park (Afternoon)
26/12	MON	Market Rasen (Afternoon)
26/12	MON	Sedgefield (Afternoon)
26/12	MON	Wetherby (Afternoon)
26/12	MON	Wincanton (Afternoon)
26/12	MON	WOLVERHAMPTON (AWT) (Afternoon)
27/12	TUE	Chepstow (Afternoon)
27/12	TUE	Kempton Park (Afternoon)
27/12	TUE	Wetherby (Afternoon)
27/12	TUE	WOLVERHAMPTON (AWT) (Afternoon)
28/12	WED	Catterick Bridge (Afternoon)
28/12	WED	Leicester (Afternoon)
28/12	WED	LINGFIELD PARK (AWT) (Afternoon)
29/12	THU	Doncaster (Afternoon)
29/12	THU	Kelso (Afternoon)
29/12	THU	SOUTHWELL (AWT) (Afternoon)
30/12	FRI	Haydock Park (Afternoon)
30/12	FRI	NEWCASTLE (AWT) (Afternoon)
30/12	FRI	Taunton (Afternoon)
31/12	SAT	LINGFIELD PARK (AWT) (Afternoon)
31/12	SAT	Newbury (Afternoon)
31/12	SAT	Uttoxeter (Afternoon)
31/12	SAT	Warwick (Afternoon)

Rugby Premier League Fixtures

(Dec 15 – May 16)

Fri 4th Dec 15	19:45	Gloucester Rugby	v	Sale Sharks
Sat 5th Dec 15	15:00	Harlequins	v	London Irish
Sat 5th Dec 15	15:00	Worcester Warriors	v	Leicester Tigers
Sat 5th Dec 15	15:15	Bath Rugby	v	Northampton Saints
Sat 5th Dec 15	17:30	Wasps	v	Exeter Chiefs
Sun 6th Dec 15	15:00	Newcastle Falcons	v	Saracens
Sat 26th Dec 15	15:00	Exeter Chiefs	v	Sale Sharks
Sat 26th Dec 15	15:00	Leicester Tigers	v	Newcastle Falcons
Sat 26th Dec 15	15:00	London Irish	v	Northampton Saints
Sat 26th Dec 15	15:15	Bath Rugby	v	Worcester Warriors
Sun 27th Dec 15	15:00	Harlequins	v	Gloucester Rugby
Sun 27th Dec 15	15:00	Wasps	v	Saracens
Sat 2nd Jan 16	14:30	Sale Sharks	v	Wasps
Sat 2nd Jan 16	15:00	Gloucester Rugby	v	London Irish
Sat 2nd Jan 16	15:00	Newcastle Falcons	v	Bath Rugby
Sat 2nd Jan 16	15:00	Northampton Saints	v	Exeter Chiefs
Sat 2nd Jan 16	15:00	Saracens	v	Leicester Tigers
Sat 2nd Jan 16	15:00	Worcester Warriors	v	Harlequins
Sat 9th Jan 16	15:00	Exeter Chiefs	v	Gloucester Rugby
Sat 9th Jan 16	15:00	Harlequins	v	Saracens

Sat 9th Jan 16	15:00	Leicester Tigers	v	Northampton Saints
Sat 9th Jan 16	15:15	Bath Rugby	v	Sale Sharks
Sun 10th Jan 16	14:00	Wasps	v	Worcester Warriors
Sun 10th Jan 16	15:00	London Irish	v	Newcastle Falcons
Sat 30th Jan 16	14:30	Sale Sharks	v	London Irish
Sat 30th Jan 16	15:00	Gloucester Rugby	v	Leicester Tigers
Sat 30th Jan 16	15:00	Northampton Saints	v	Wasps
Sat 30th Jan 16	15:00	Saracens	v	Bath Rugby
Sat 30th Jan 16	15:00	Worcester Warriors	v	Exeter Chiefs
Sun 31st Jan 16	15:00	Newcastle Falcons	v	Harlequins
Sat 6th Feb 16	14:00	Wasps	v	Newcastle Falcons
Sat 6th Feb 16	15:00	Exeter Chiefs	v	Saracens
Sat 6th Feb 16	15:00	Harlequins	v	Northampton Saints
Sat 6th Feb 16	15:00	Leicester Tigers	v	Sale Sharks
Sat 6th Feb 16	15:15	Bath Rugby	v	Gloucester Rugby
Sun 7th Feb 16	13:00	London Irish	v	Worcester Warriors
Sat 13th Feb 16	14:30	Sale Sharks	v	Exeter Chiefs
Sat 13th Feb 16	15:00	Gloucester Rugby	v	Harlequins
Sat 13th Feb 16	15:00	Northampton Saints	v	London Irish
Sat 13th Feb 16	15:00	Saracens	v	Wasps
Sat 13th Feb 16	15:00	Worcester Warriors	v	Bath Rugby
Sun 14th Feb 16	16:00	Newcastle Falcons	v	Leicester Tigers
Sat 20th Feb 16	15:00	Harlequins	v	Leicester Tigers

Sat 20th Feb 16	15:00	London Irish	v	Exeter Chiefs
Sat 20th Feb 16	15:00	Saracens	v	Gloucester Rugby
Sat 20th Feb 16	15:00	Worcester Warriors	v	Sale Sharks
Sat 20th Feb 16	15:15	Bath Rugby	v	Wasps
Sun 21st Feb 16	15:00	Newcastle Falcons	v	Northampton Saints
Sat 27th Feb 16	14:30	Sale Sharks	v	Saracens
Sat 27th Feb 16	15:00	Exeter Chiefs	v	Bath Rugby
Sat 27th Feb 16	15:00	Gloucester Rugby	v	Newcastle Falcons
Sat 27th Feb 16	15:00	Leicester Tigers	v	London Irish
Sat 27th Feb 16	15:00	Northampton Saints	v	Worcester Warriors
Sun 28th Feb 16	14:00	Wasps	v	Harlequins
Fri 4th Mar 16	20:00	Newcastle Falcons	v	Worcester Warriors
Sat 5th Mar 16	14:30	Sale Sharks	v	Harlequins
Sat 5th Mar 16	15:00	Gloucester Rugby	v	Wasps
Sat 5th Mar 16	15:00	Leicester Tigers	v	Exeter Chiefs
Sat 5th Mar 16	15:00	Saracens	v	Northampton Saints
Sat 5th Mar 16	15:15	Bath Rugby	v	London Irish
Sat 12th Mar 16	14:00	Northampton Saints	v	Sale Sharks
Sat 12th Mar 16	14:00	Wasps	v	Leicester Tigers
Sat 12th Mar 16	15:00	Exeter Chiefs	v	Newcastle Falcons
Sat 12th Mar 16	15:00	Harlequins	v	Bath Rugby
Sat 12th Mar 16	15:00	London Irish	v	Saracens
Sat 12th Mar 16	15:00	Worcester Warriors	v	Gloucester Rugby

Sat 19th Mar 16	15:00	Exeter Chiefs	v	Northampton Saints
Sat 19th Mar 16	15:00	Harlequins	v	Worcester Warriors
Sat 19th Mar 16	15:00	Leicester Tigers	v	Saracens
Sat 19th Mar 16	15:15	Bath Rugby	v	Newcastle Falcons
Sun 20th Mar 16	14:00	Wasps	v	Sale Sharks
Sun 20th Mar 16	15:00	London Irish	v	Gloucester Rugby
Sat 26th Mar 16	14:30	Sale Sharks	v	Leicester Tigers
Sat 26th Mar 16	15:00	Gloucester Rugby	v	Bath Rugby
Sat 26th Mar 16	15:00	Northampton Saints	v	Harlequins
Sat 26th Mar 16	15:00	Saracens	v	Exeter Chiefs
Sat 26th Mar 16	15:00	Worcester Warriors	v	London Irish
Sun 27th Mar 16	15:00	Newcastle Falcons	v	Wasps
Sat 2nd Apr 16	15:00	Exeter Chiefs	v	Worcester Warriors
Sat 2nd Apr 16	15:00	Harlequins	v	Newcastle Falcons
Sat 2nd Apr 16	15:00	Leicester Tigers	v	Gloucester Rugby
Sat 2nd Apr 16	15:00	London Irish	v	Sale Sharks
Sat 2nd Apr 16	15:00	Wasps	v	Northampton Saints
Sat 2nd Apr 16	15:15	Bath Rugby	v	Saracens
Sat 16th Apr 16	14:30	Sale Sharks	v	Bath Rugby
Sat 16th Apr 16	15:00	Gloucester Rugby	v	Exeter Chiefs
Sat 16th Apr 16	15:00	Northampton Saints	v	Leicester Tigers
Sat 16th Apr 16	15:00	Saracens	v	Harlequins
Sat 16th Apr 16	15:00	Worcester Warriors	v	Wasps

Sun 17th Apr 16	15:00	Newcastle Falcons	v	London Irish
Sat 30th Apr 16	14:30	Sale Sharks	v	Gloucester Rugby
Sat 30th Apr 16	15:00	Exeter Chiefs	v	Wasps
Sat 30th Apr 16	15:00	Leicester Tigers	v	Worcester Warriors
Sat 30th Apr 16	15:00	Northampton Saints	v	Bath Rugby
Sat 30th Apr 16	15:00	Saracens	v	Newcastle Falcons
Sun 1st May 16	15:00	London Irish	v	Harlequins
Sat 7th May 16	TBA	Bath	v	Leicester Tigers
Sat 7th May 16	TBA	Gloucester	v	Northampton Saints
Sat 7th May 16	TBA	Quins	v	Exeter Chiefs
Sat 7th May 16	TBA	Falcons	v	Sale Sharks
Sat 7th May 16	TBA	Wasps	v	London Irish
Sat 7th May 16	TBA	Worcester	v	Saracens

2016 Six Nations fixtures

Saturday 6th February – France v Italy (2.25pm GMT unless stated)
Saturday 6th February – Scotland v England (4.50pm)
Sunday 7th February – Ireland v Wales (3pm)

Saturday 13th February – France v Ireland (2.25pm)
Saturday 13th February – Wales v Scotland (4.50pm)
Sunday 14th February – Italy v England (2pm)

Friday 26th February – Wales v France (8.05pm)
Saturday 27th February – Italy v Scotland (2.25pm)
Saturday 27th February – England v Ireland (4.50pm)

Saturday 12th March - Ireland v Italy (1.30pm)
Saturday 12th March – England v Wales (4pm)
Sunday 13th March – Scotland v France (3pm)

Saturday 19th March – Wales v Italy (2.30pm)
Saturday 19th March – Ireland v Scotland (5pm)
Saturday 19th March – France v England (8pm)

Grand Slams

18 January – 31 January 2016
Australian Open

22 May – 5 June 2016
French Open

27 June to - 10 July 2016
Wimbledon

29 August 2016 – 12 September 2016
U.S. Open

Tournament List

January 2016
4th - 10th ATP Brisbane International presented by Suncorp, Brisbane, Australia.
4th - 10th ATP Aircel Chennai Open, Chennai, India.
4th - 10th ATP Qatar ExxonMobil Open, Doha, Qatar.
11th - 17th ATP Heineken Open, Auckland, New Zealand.
11th - 17th ATP Apia International Sydney, Sydney, Australia.
18th - 31st Australian Open, Melboune, Australia.

February 2016

1st - 7th ATP PBZ Zagreb Indoors, Zagreb, Croatia.

1st - 7th ATP Open Sud de France, Montpellier, France.

1st - 7th ATP Ecuador Open Quito, Quito, Ecuador.

8th - 14th ATP ABN AMRO World Tennis Tournament, Rotterdam, Netherlands.

8th - 14th ATP Memphis Open, Memphis, Tennessee, United States of America.

8th - 14th ATP Argentina Open, Buenos Aires, Argentina.

15th - 21st ATP Delray Beach Open, Delray Beach, Florida, United States of America.

15th - 21st ATP Open 13, Marseille, France.

15th - 21st ATP Rio Open presented by Claro, Rio de Janeiro, Brazil.

22nd - 28th ATP Abierto Mexicano Telcel, Acapulco, Mexico.

22nd - 28th ATP Brasil Open, Sao Paulo, Brazil.

22nd - 28th ATP Dubai Duty Free Tennis Championships, Dubai, United Arab Emirates.

29th - 2nd March Davis Cup First Round, TBD.

March 2016

7th - 20th ATP BNP Paribas Open, Indian Wells, California, United States of America.

21st - 4th April ATP Miami Open presented by Itau, Miami, Florida, United States of America.

April 2016

4th - 10th ATP Grand Prix Hassan II, Casablanca, Morocco.

4th - 10th ATP Fayez Sarofim & Co. US Men's Clay Court Championships, Houston, Texas, United States of America.

11th - 17th ATP Monte-Carlo Rolex Masters, Monte-Carlo, Monaco.

18th - 24th ATP Barcelona Open BancSabadell, Barcelona, Spain.

18th - 24th ATP BRD Nastase Tiriac Trophy, Bucharest, Romania.

25th - 1st May ATP Millennium Estoril Open, Estoril, Portugal.

25th - 1st May ATP TEB BNP Paribas Istanbul Open, Istanbul, Turkey.
25th - 1st May ATP BMW Open by FWU AG, Munich, Germany.

May 2016
2nd - 8th ATP Mutua Madrid Open, Madrid, Spain.
9th - 15th ATP International BNL d'Italia, Rome, Italy.
16th - 22nd ATP Geneva Open, Geneva, Switzerland.
16th - 22nd ATP Open de Nice Cote d'Azur, Nice, France.
22nd - 5th June French Open, Roland Garros, Paris, France.

June 2016
6th - 12th ATP Mercedes Cup, Stuttgart, Germany.
6th - 12th ATP Topshelf Open, 's-Hertogenbosch, Netherlands.
13th - 19th ATP Aegon Championships, London, England.
13th - 19th ATP Gerry Weber Open, Halle, Germany.
20th - 26th ATP Aegon Open Nottingham, Nottingham, England.
27th - 10th July The All England Lawn Tennis Championships, Wimbledon, London, England.

July 2016
11th - 17th ATP Hall of Fame Tennis Championships, Newport, Rhode Island, United States of America.
11th - 17th ATP bet-at-home Open, Hamburg, Germany.
11th - 13th Davis Cup Quarter-Finals, TBD.
11th - 17th ATP SkiStar Swedish Open, Bastad, Sweden.
18th - 24th ATP Suisse Open Gstaad, Gstaad, Switzerland.
18th - 24th ATP Generali Open, Kitzbuhel, Austria.
18th - 24th ATP Konzum Croatia Open Umag, Umag, Croatia.
18th - 24th ATP Citi Open, Washington D.C, United States of America.
25th - 31st ATP Rogers Cup, Toronto, Canada.

August 2016
1st - 7th ATP BB&T Atlanta Open, Atlanta, Georgia, United States of America.
8th - 14th ATP Claro Open Colombia, Bogota, Colombia.

15th - 21st ATP Western & Southern Open, Cincinnati, Ohio, United States of America.

22nd - 28th ATP Winston-Salem Open, Winston-Salem, North Carolina, United States of America.

29th - 12th September US Open, Flushing Meadows, New York, United States of America

THE 4 MAJORS

THE MASTERS
4th - 11th April 2016

U.S. OPEN
13th – 19th June 2016

OPEN CHAMPIONSHIP
10th – 17th July 2016

PGA CHAMPIONSHIP
25th – 31st July 2016

Past Winners (The Masters)

2008 Trevor Immelman

2009 Ángel Cabrera

2010 Phil Mickelson

2011 Charl Schwartzel

2012 Bubba Watson

2013 Adam Scott

2014 Bubba Watson

2015 Jordan Spieth

Golf Past Winners (U.S. OPEN)

2008 Tiger Woods

2009 Lucas Glover

2010 Graeme McDowell

2011 Rory McIlroy

2012 Webb Simpson

2013 Justin Rose

2014 Martin Kaymer

2015 Jordan Spieth

Past Winners (THE. OPEN CHAMPIONSHIP)

2008 Pádraig Harrington

2009 Stewart Cink

2010 Louis Oosthuizen

2011 Darren Clarke

2012 Ernie Els

2013 Phil Mickelson

2014 Rory McIlroy

2015 Zach Johnson

2008 Pádraig Harrington

2009 Yang Yong-eun

2010 Martin Kaymer

2011 Keegan Bradley

2012 Rory McIlroy

2013 Jason Dufner

2014 Rory McIlroy

2015 Jason Day

OTHER GOLF TOURNAMENTS

Jan. 7-10
PGA Tour: Hyundai Tournament of Champions
Kapalua Resort (Plantation Course)
Kapalua, Hawaii

Jan. 14-17
PGA Tour: Sony Open in Hawaii
Waialae Country Club
Honolulu, Hawai

Jan. 21-24
PGA Tour: Career Builder Challenge
PGA West (Stadium Course, Nicklaus Tournament Course) and La
Quinta Country Club
La Quinta, Calif.

Jan. 28-31
PGA Tour: Farmers Insurance Open
Torrey Pines Golf Course (South Course, North Course)
La Jolla, Calif.

Feb. 4-7
PGA Tour: Waste Management Phoenix Open
TPC Scottsdale (Stadium Course)
Scottsdale, Ariz.

Feb. 11-14
PGA Tour: AT&T Pebble Beach National Pro-Am
Pebble Beach Golf Links, Spyglass Hill Golf Course, Monterey
Peninsula Country Club (Shore Course)
Pebble Beach, Calif.

Feb. 18-21
PGA Tour: Northern Trust Open
Riviera Country Club
Pacific Palisades, Calif.

Feb. 25-28
PGA Tour: Honda Classic
PGA National (Champion Course)
Palm Beach Gardens, Fla.

Mar. 3-6
PGA Tour/European Tour: WGC-Cadillac Championship
Trump National Doral (Blue Monster Course)
Doral, Fla.

Mar. 10-13
PGA Tour: Valspar Championship
Innisbrook Resort and Golf Club (Copperhead Course)
Palm Harbor, Fla.

Mar. 17-20
PGA Tour: Arnold Palmer Invitational
Bay Hill Golf Club and Lodge
Orlando, Fla.

Mar. 24-27
PGA Tour/European Tour: WGC-Dell Match Play
Austin Country Club
Austin, Texas

Mar. 24-27
PGA Tour: Puerto Rico Open
Coco Beach Golf and Country Club
Rio Grande, Puerto Rico

Mar. 31-April 3
Shell Houston Open
Golf Club of Houston (Tournament Course)
Humble, Texas

April 7-10
PGA Tour: Masters Tournament
Augusta National Golf Club
Augusta, Ga.

April 14-17
PGA Tour: RBC Heritage
Harbour Town Golf Links
Hilton Head Island, S.C.

April 21-24
PGA Tour: Valero Texas Open
TPC San Antonio (AT&T Oaks Course)
San Antonio, Texas

April 28-May 1
PGA Tour: Zurich Classic of New Orleans
TPC Louisiana
New Orleans, La.

May 5-8
PGA Tour: Wells Fargo Championship
Quail Hollow Club
Charlotte, N.C.

May 12-15
PGA Tour: Players Championship
TPC Sawgrass (The Players Stadium Course)
Ponte Vedra Beach, Fla.

May 19-22
PGA Tour: AT&T Byron Nelson
Four Seasons Resort and Club Dallas at Las Colinas (TPC Four
Seasons Las Colinas)
Irving, Texas

May 26-29
PGA Tour: Colonial National Invitational Tournament
Colonial Country Club
Fort Worth, Texas

June 2-5
PGA Tour: Memorial Tournament
Muirfield Village Golf Club
Dublin, Ohio

June 9-12
PGA Tour: FedEx St. Jude Classic
TPC Southwind
Memphis, Tenn.

June 16-19
PGA Tour: U.S. Open
Oakmont Country Club
Oakmont, Pa.

June 23-26
PGA Tour: Quicken Loans National
Congressional Country Club
Bethesda, Md.

June 30-July 3
PGA Tour/European Tour: WGC-Bridgestone Invitational
Firestone Country Club (South Course)
Akron, Ohio

June 30-July 3
PGA Tour: Barracuda Championship
Montreux Golf and Country Club
Reno, Nev.

July 7-10
PGA Tour: Greenbrier Classic
The Greenbrier (The Old White TPC)
White Sulphur Springs, W. Va.

July 14-17
European Tour: Open Championship
Royal Troon Golf Club
Troon, Scotland

July 14-17
PGA Tour: Barbasol Championship
Robert Trent Jones Trail (Grand National Lake Course)
Opelika, Ala.

July 21-24
PGA Tour: RBC Canadian Open
Glen Abbey Golf Club
Oakville, Ontario

July 28-31
PGA of America: PGA Championship
Baltusrol Golf Club (Lower Course)
Springfield, N.J.

Aug. 4-7
PGA Tour: Travelers Championship
TPC River Highlands
Cromwell, Conn.

Aug. 11-14
PGA Tour: John Deere Classic
TPC Deere Run
Silvis, Ill.

Aug. 11-14
Olympics: Men's Golf Competition
Olympic Golf Course
Rio de Janeiro, Brazil

Aug. 18-21
PGA Tour: Wyndham Championship
Sedgefield Country Club
Greensboro, N.C.

Aug. 25-28
PGA Tour: The Barclays
Bethpage State Park (Black Course)
Bethpage, N.Y.

Sept. 2-5
PGA Tour: Deutsche Bank Championship
TPC Boston
Norton, Mass.

Sept. 8-11
PGA Tour: BMW Championship
Crooked Stick Golf Club
Carmel, Ind.

Sept. 22-25
PGA Tour: Tour Championship
East Lake Golf Club
Atlanta, Ga.

Sept. 30-Oct. 2
Ryder Cup
Hazeltine National Golf Club
Chaska, Minn.

Monday 28 December
Barclays Premier League
15:00 Arsenal v. Bournemouth
15:00 Crystal Palace v. Swansea City
15:00 Everton v. Stoke City
15:00 Leicester City v. Manchester City
15:00 Manchester United v. Chelsea
15:00 Norwich City v. Aston Villa
15:00 Sunderland v. Liverpool
15:00 Watford v. Tottenham Hotspur
15:00 West Bromwich Albion v. Newcastle United
15:00 West Ham United v. Southampton

Saturday 2 January
Barclays Premier League
15:00 Arsenal v. Newcastle United
15:00 Crystal Palace v. Chelsea
15:00 Everton v. Tottenham Hotspur
15:00 Leicester City v. Bournemouth
15:00 Manchester United v. Swansea City
 15:00 Norwich City v. Southampton
15:00 Sunderland v. Aston Villa
15:00 Watford v. Manchester City
15:00 West Bromwich Albion v. Stoke City
15:00 West Ham United v. Liverpool

Tuesday 12 January
Barclays Premier League
19:45Aston Villa v. Crystal Palace
19:45Bournemouth v. West Ham United
19:45Swansea City v. Sunderland
20:00 Liverpool v. Arsenal

Wednesday 13 January
Barclays Premier League
19:45Chelsea v. West Bromwich Albion
19:45Manchester City v. Everton
19:45Newcastle United v. Manchester United
19:45Southampton v. Watford
19:45Stoke City v. Norwich City
20:00 Tottenham Hotspur v. Leicester City

Saturday 16 January
Barclays Premier League
15:00 Aston Villa v. Leicester City
15:00 Bournemouth v. Norwich City
15:00 Chelsea v. Everton
15:00 Liverpool v. Manchester United
15:00 Manchester City v. Crystal Palace
15:00 Newcastle United v. West Ham United
15:00 Southampton v. West Bromwich Albion
15:00 Stoke City v. Arsenal
15:00 Swansea City v. Watford
15:00 Tottenham Hotspur v. Sunderland

Saturday 23 January
Barclays Premier League
15:00 Arsenal v. Chelsea
15:00 Crystal Palace v. Tottenham Hotspur
15:00 Everton v. Swansea City
15:00 Leicester City v. Stoke City
15:00 Manchester United v. Southampton
15:00 Norwich City v. Liverpool
15:00 Sunderland v. Bournemouth
15:00 Watford v. Newcastle United
15:00 West Bromwich Albion v. Aston Villa
15:00 West Ham United v. Manchester City

Tuesday 2 February
Barclays Premier League
19:45Arsenal v. Southampton
19:45Leicester City v. Liverpool
19:45Norwich City v. Tottenham Hotspur
19:45Sunderland v. Manchester City
19:45Watford v. Chelsea
19:45West Ham United v. Aston Villa
20:00 Crystal Palace v. Bournemouth
20:00 Manchester United v. Stoke City
20:00 West Bromwich Albion v. Swansea City

Wednesday 3 February
Barclays Premier League
19:45 Everton v. Newcastle United

Saturday 6 February
Barclays Premier League
15:00 Aston Villa v. Norwich City
15:00 Bournemouth v. Arsenal
15:00 Chelsea v. Manchester United
15:00 Liverpool v. Sunderland
15:00 Manchester City v. Leicester City
15:00 Newcastle United v. West Bromwich Albion
15:00 Southampton v. West Ham United
15:00 Stoke City v. Everton
15:00 Swansea City v. Crystal Palace
15:00 Tottenham Hotspur v. Watford

Saturday 13 February
Barclays Premier League
15:00 Arsenal v. Leicester City
15:00 Aston Villa v. Liverpool
15:00 Bournemouth v. Stoke City
15:00 Chelsea v. Newcastle United
15:00 Crystal Palace v. Watford
15:00 Everton v. West Bromwich Albion
15:00 Manchester City v. Tottenham Hotspur
15:00 Norwich City v. West Ham United
15:00 Sunderland v. Manchester United
15:00 Swansea City v. Southampton

Saturday 27 February
Barclays Premier League
15:00 Leicester City v. Norwich City
15:00 Liverpool v. Everton
15:00 Manchester United v. Arsenal
15:00 Newcastle United v. Manchester City
15:00 Southampton v. Chelsea
15:00 Stoke City v. Aston Villa
15:00 Tottenham Hotspur v. Swansea City
15:00 Watford v. Bournemouth
15:00 West Bromwich Albion v. Crystal Palace
15:00 West Ham United v. Sunderland

Tuesday 1 March
Barclays Premier League
19:45Arsenal v. Swansea City
19:45Aston Villa v. Everton
19:45Bournemouth v. Southampton
19:45Leicester City v. West Bromwich Albion
19:45Norwich City v. Chelsea
19:45Sunderland v. Crystal Palace
19:45West Ham United v. Tottenham Hotspur 20:00
Liverpool v. Manchester City
20:00 Manchester United v. Watford

Wednesday 2 March
Barclays Premier League
19:45 Stoke City v. Newcastle United

Saturday 5 March
Barclays Premier League
15:00 Chelsea v. Stoke City
15:00 Crystal Palace v. Liverpool
15:00 Everton v. West Ham United
15:00 Manchester City v. Aston Villa
15:00 Newcastle United v. Bournemouth
15:00 Southampton v. Sunderland
15:00 Swansea City v. Norwich City
15:00 Tottenham Hotspur v. Arsenal
15:00 Watford v. Leicester City
15:00 West Bromwich Albion v. Manchester United

Saturday 12 March
Barclays Premier League
15:00 Arsenal v. West Bromwich Albion
15:00 Aston Villa v. Tottenham Hotspur
15:00 Bournemouth v. Swansea City
15:00 Leicester City v. Newcastle United
15:00 Liverpool v. Chelsea
15:00 Manchester United v. Crystal Palace
15:00 Norwich City v. Manchester City
15:00 Stoke City v. Southampton
15:00 Sunderland v. Everton
15:00 West Ham United v. Watford

Saturday 19 March
Barclays Premier League
15:00 Chelsea v. West Ham United
15:00 Crystal Palace v. Leicester City
15:00 Everton v. Arsenal
15:00 Manchester City v. Manchester United
15:00 Newcastle United v. Sunderland
15:00 Southampton v. Liverpool
15:00 Swansea City v. Aston Villa
15:00 Tottenham Hotspur v. Bournemouth
15:00 Watford v. Stoke City
15:00 West Bromwich Albion v. Norwich City

Saturday 2 April
Barclays Premier League
15:00 Arsenal v. Watford
15:00 Aston Villa v. Chelsea
15:00 Bournemouth v. Manchester City
15:00 Leicester City v. Southampton
15:00 Liverpool v. Tottenham Hotspur
15:00 Manchester United v. Everton
15:00 Norwich City v. Newcastle United
15:00 Stoke City v. Swansea City
15:00 Sunderland v. West Bromwich Albion
15:00 West Ham United v. Crystal Palace

Saturday 9 April
Barclays Premier League
15:00 Aston Villa v. Bournemouth
15:00 Crystal Palace v. Norwich City
15:00 Liverpool v. Stoke City
15:00 Manchester City v. West Bromwich Albion
15:00 Southampton v. Newcastle United
15:00 Sunderland v. Leicester City
15:00 Swansea City v. Chelsea
15:00 Tottenham Hotspur v. Manchester United
15:00 Watford v. Everton
15:00 West Ham United v. Arsenal

Saturday 16 April
Barclays Premier League
15:00 Arsenal v. Crystal Palace
15:00 Bournemouth v. Liverpool
15:00 Chelsea v. Manchester City
15:00 Everton v. Southampton
15:00 Leicester City v. West Ham United
15:00 Manchester United v. Aston Villa
15:00 Newcastle United v. Swansea City
15:00 Norwich City v. Sunderland
15:00 Stoke City v. Tottenham Hotspur
15:00 West Bromwich Albion v. Watford

Saturday 23 April

Barclays Premier League

15:00 Aston Villa v. Southampton

15:00 Bournemouth v. Chelsea

15:00 Crystal Palace v. Everton

15:00 Leicester City v. Swansea City

15:00 Liverpool v. Newcastle United

15:00 Manchester City v. Stoke City

15:00 Norwich City v. Watford

15:00 Sunderland v. Arsenal

15:00 Tottenham Hotspur v. West Bromwich Albion

15:00 West Ham United v. Manchester United

Saturday 30 April

Barclays Premier League

15:00 Arsenal v. Norwich City

15:00 Chelsea v. Tottenham Hotspur

15:00 Everton v. Bournemouth

15:00 Manchester United v. Leicester City

15:00 Newcastle United v. Crystal Palace

15:00 Southampton v. Manchester City

15:00 Stoke City v. Sunderland

15:00 Swansea City v. Liverpool

15:00 Watford v. Aston Villa

15:00 West Bromwich Albion v. West Ham United

Saturday 7 May
Barclays Premier League
15:00 Aston Villa v. Newcastle United
15:00 Bournemouth v. West Bromwich Albion
15:00 Crystal Palace v. Stoke City
15:00 Leicester City v. Everton
15:00 Liverpool v. Watford
15:00 Manchester City v. Arsenal
15:00 Norwich City v. Manchester United
15:00 Sunderland v. Chelsea
15:00 Tottenham Hotspur v. Southampton
15:00 West Ham United v. Swansea City

Sunday 15 May
Barclays Premier League
15:00 Arsenal v. Aston Villa
15:00 Chelsea v. Leicester City
15:00 Everton v. Norwich City
15:00 Manchester United v. Bournemouth
15:00 Newcastle United v. Tottenham Hotspur
15:00 Southampton v. Crystal Palace
15:00 Stoke City v. West Ham United
15:00 Swansea City v. Manchester City
15:00 Watford v. Sunderland
15:00 West Bromwich Albion v. Liverpool

IMPORTANT FOOTBALL CUP FIXTURES

<u>Important Cups</u>

Sunday 28th February 2016 – LEAGUE CUP FINAL

Saturday 21st May 2016 – FA CUP FINAL

Wednesday 18th May 2016 –
 UEFA EUROPA LEAGUE FINAL

Saturday 28th May 2016 – CHAMPIONS LEAGUE FINAL

EURO 2016 - FRANCE

Friday 10th June 2016 – 10th July 2016

Yearly Planner

	M	T	W	T	F	S	S	M	T	W	T	F	S	S	M	T	W	T	F	S	S	M	T	W	T	F	S	S	M	T	W	T	F	S	S	M	T
Jan					1	2	3	4	5	6	7	8	9	10	11	12	13	14	15	16	17	18	19	20	21	22	23	24	25	26	27	28	29	30	31		
Feb	1	2	3	4	5	6	7	8	9	10	11	12	13	14	15	16	17	18	19	20	21	22	23	24	25	26	27	28	29								
Mar		1	2	3	4	5	6	7	8	9	10	11	12	13	14	15	16	17	18	19	20	21	22	23	24	25	26	27	28	29	30	31					
Apr					1	2	3	4	5	6	7	8	9	10	11	12	13	14	15	16	17	18	19	20	21	22	23	24	25	26	27	28	29	30			
May							1	2	3	4	5	6	7	8	9	10	11	12	13	14	15	16	17	18	19	20	21	22	23	24	25	26	27	28	29	30	31
Jun			1	2	3	4	5	6	7	8	9	10	11	12	13	14	15	16	17	18	19	20	21	22	23	24	25	26	27	28	29	30					
Jul					1	2	3	4	5	6	7	8	9	10	11	12	13	14	15	16	17	18	19	20	21	22	23	24	25	26	27	28	29	30	31		
Aug	1	2	3	4	5	6	7	8	9	10	11	12	13	14	15	16	17	18	19	20	21	22	23	24	25	26	27	28	29	30	31						
Sept				1	2	3	4	5	6	7	8	9	10	11	12	13	14	15	16	17	18	19	20	21	22	23	24	25	26	27	28	29	30				
Oct						1	2	3	4	5	6	7	8	9	10	11	12	13	14	15	16	17	18	19	20	21	22	23	24	25	26	27	28	29	30	31	
Nov		1	2	3	4	5	6	7	8	9	10	11	12	13	14	15	16	17	18	19	20	21	22	23	24	25	26	27	28	29	30						
Dec				1	2	3	4	5	6	7	8	9	10	11	12	13	14	15	16	17	18	19	20	21	22	23	24	25	26	27	28	29	30	31			

Public Holidays in England and Wales in 2016

New Year's Day	January 1
Good Friday	March 25
Easter Monday	March 28
Early May Bank Holiday	May 2
Spring Bank Holiday	May 30
Summer Bank Holiday	August 29
Boxing Day	December 26
Christmas Day Holiday	December 27

Personal Blank Chart Of Sport Or Training

Date	Time or Score	Event/ Description

Date	Time or Score	Event/ Description

CPSIA information can be obtained at www.ICGtesting.com
Printed in the USA
LVOW10s1956301215

468476LV00022B/1089/P